THE
ESCAPE
TO
FREEDOM

Copyright © 2011 by Jona Goldrich
All rights reserved.

ISBN-10: 1463797788
EAN-13: 9781463797782

THE ESCAPE TO FREEDOM

AUTHORED BY
MEIR DORON & SHANNA MAIMON,
RETOLD BY JONA GOLDRICH,
EDITED BY JULIE BEERS

Dedicated to my mother, my father, and my brother, Eizo
God bless their souls

And in the memory of all my family members who
perished in the Holocaust

To my brother, Bumek

To my wife Doretta

To my daughters Melinda and Andrea

To my grandchildren – Garrett, Lindsay and Derek

And for all the following generations –
In hope that they will remember
and learn from the past for a promising future

The Escape to Freedom

PROLOGUE

1992 – Yona Goldrich (formerly Goldreich) and his younger brother, Bumek (Avraham), stood in front of their childhood home in Turka, on the border between Poland and Ukraine. Half a century had passed since the brothers last stood on Polish soil but suddenly time seemed to vanish. In his mind, Yona was once again a boy, nearly fifteen. World War II raged around them and Turka was under Nazi control.

On a bitter day in the summer of 1942, Yona's mother hugged him tightly. She could hardly bear to let Yona and Bumek out of her embrace. Urgently, Yona's father hastened the boys' goodbyes to their parents and older brother, Eizo. It was time for the children to try their daring escape to Hungary with a smuggler. Yona shouldered the knapsack his parents packed with food for the road, some clothes and a couple of gold chains and diamond rings in hidden pockets. Yona also shouldered the responsibility for watching over his thirteen-year-old brother until the rest of the family was smuggled out in the next couple of weeks.

Yona took his younger brother's hand and they ran – moving from one uncertain situation to another. Death haunted them at every turn. Life for the boys was a desperate struggle to survive and a constant, heartbreaking search to reunite with their family.

Now that the Iron Curtain in Eastern Europe had been lifted, Yona and Bumek returned home. Three cousins – Meir (Manek), Itzhak (Eizo) and Steven Hirth – joined the brothers on this emotional journey. They bribed the Mayor and the Chief of Police to help them find the building. It was still standing, having survived time and war. The tile roof, the heavy wooden door and the wide-open windows were just as Yona remembered. In Yona's childhood memories, his home, with its five rooms, was large and spacious. Now, in the eyes of a successful real-estate entrepreneur from Los Angeles, the house looked grey and small.

Yona looked from the outside into the "spacious" children's room he had shared with his two brothers. He could only chuckle as he compared it to the large rooms his two daughters, Melinda and Andrea, grew up in. Yona's children also had running water and electricity, which were rare during Yona's childhood in Turka. And, of course, his daughters never had to leave the main building to use the lavatory in the backyard near the river. Yona smiled at the flood of memories of a peaceful and happy childhood before the war.

For a long moment, Yona stood in front of his house. He craved to go inside, to inhale the air, close his eyes and experience again the years of his childhood. He longed to be immersed in the warm embrace of his mother, Elza; to be surrounded by his father, Sender, and his two brothers, Eizo and Bumek.

More than anything, Yona hoped the new residents of the house had found and kept the family's photo album. Indeed, this treasured remnant of his family might still be in its secret hiding place. Yona and Bumek approached the front door, hoping to find this link to the enchanted years of their childhood. The last time the brothers stood on this doorstep, their world had been turned upside down with unspeakable violence. Yona knocked and waited for the door to his past to open.

CHAPTER ONE

Yona Goldreich was born on September 11, 1927 in Turka, a small town in the district of Lvov (Lemberg) in eastern Poland (now in the Ukraine). The town is situated at the foot of the Carpathian Mountains, not far from the sources of the river Dniester, which flows into the Black Sea.

Jews first arrived in Turka in 1730, almost two hundred years before Yona was born. A short time after the small village became a town, Nobleman Kalinovsky, the lord of the region, invited twenty-five Jewish families to settle in Turka. Kalinovsky understood well enough that without Jews, who were known as merchants and educated people, Turka could not function properly as a town. In order to attract Jews to make a life in Turka, Kalinovsky built the first synagogue there, opened a Jewish hostel, and provided a parcel of land to be used as a Jewish cemetery. And it was mainly due to the arrival of Jews that Turka expanded and increased the number of its inhabitants.

Life in Turka and its surroundings was simple, almost primitive. The climate was not easy either. Summer days were enjoyable but wintertime was ice cold, and the town was covered in heavy snow for many months.

Among those who settled in the district of Turka was Shraga Fattal Goldreich, Yona's paternal grandfather. He was the descendant of Jews from Spain who had been expelled from their country in the 15th century and scattered across Europe, embracing new family names. Usually they chose names based on their professions: A tailor became Mr. Schneider, a shoemaker became Mr. Schumacher. Those who could afford it, paid for a name they could choose themselves. Shraga Fattal's forefathers had acquired an honorable name, one that would open doors, "Goldreich," meaning "gold" or "wealth."

Shraga Fattal took advantage of the historic legislation of the Austro-Hungarian Emperor, Franz Joseph II, allowing Jews to buy land for the first time. Until then, it had been forbidden for Jews to own property and accumulate assets. He acquired a fertile piece of land in Botelka, a village near Turka, and built a prosperous farm. In the center of the estate, he erected a flourmill and grew potatoes in the surrounding fields. One of the reasons for his success was his compensation system: instead of paying salaries, he gave his workers a percentage of the produce.

Shraga Fattal and his wife, Naomi, raised twelve children, eight sons and four daughters. Sender (Alexander) Goldreich, born in 1892, was their first-born son.

Shraga became very successful in the farming business. His economic status allowed him to hire the services of a rabbi who lived on the farm, and served as a private tutor for the Jewish education Shraga provided to his sons.

In 1902, Turka was connected to the national railway system, which went as far as the Hungarian capital, Budapest. Turka attracted even more business, and a greater number of Jews. Additional synagogues were opened and rabbis started forming their own Chassidic communities. Jewish life prospered, until the eve of Rosh Hashanah, the Jewish New Year, in 1914. World War I erupted. Sender Goldreich, who was twenty-two-years-old at the time, was drafted into the Austro-Hungarian army.

The world of Turka's Jews collapsed overnight. The Russians quickly occupied the town, which was near the Ukrainian border. The Jews became scapegoats, accused of armed opposition to the occupying forces. The punishment inflicted by the Russians was harsh: The town's Jewish quarter was burned down. Jewish shops and homes were looted. Those who made it out in time left everything behind. Those who remained – thirty-five Jewish men, women and children – were murdered in cold blood by the Russians and their local Ukrainian collaborators.

Turka's Jews disappeared. All around, the war continued with all its might. A year later soldiers of the Austro-Hungarian Monarchy took Turka again. Only then did the Jews come out of their hiding places and return to the town. The families arrived one by one, and started to rebuild their lives and restore their homes and assets.

After World War I, the Treaty of Versailles* redefined new borders in Europe, and the status of its minority populations. Hope rose among Eastern European Jews. Poland, a new country founded on the ruins of the war, had the world's largest Jewish population, approximately 3.4 million people. Polish Jews were granted autonomy and recognized as a national entity with the right to speak Hebrew and Yiddish. They were given the right to vote and the right to be represented in all the legislative authorities of the country. They were promised freedom of religion, education and culture, and even the right to immigrate to Palestine.

Turka's Jews were included in the new country, and enjoyed equal civil rights for the first time in their history. A large and active Jewish community reemerged as a wave of Jewish newcomers arrived. Turka grew to nearly ten thousand inhabitants.

---

* World War I ended with Germany's economic and military defeat, without Germany being conquered. The Treaty of Versailles was a peace agreement between Germany and the Allies – the United States, Great Britain, France and Italy. It was signed on June 28, 1919 at the Versailles Palace on the outskirts of Paris.

When Sender returned from the battlefield, he decided not to go back to his father's farm but to make his life in the "big city," Turka. The Jewish community in Turka was typical of Eastern Europe, a "shtetl" with some five thousand residents. Most were simple people of little means who struggled every day to make a living and get their next meal. There were also Yeshiva students and a handful of "gentry," wealthy Jews in whose homes Jewish scholars dwelled and where the town's poor lined up seeking charity.

Like most Jews in Turka and the surrounding areas, the Goldreich family were orthodox Jews, graduates of Yeshivas (centers of Jewish studies), with beards and side locks. Nevertheless, the process of moving away from religion and the transition to a secular lifestyle that came in the wake of the democratization after World War I, did not skip the Goldreich family. The more they focused on their work and became proud of their success in business, the more they distanced themselves from the strictly religious lifestyle. Increasingly, they began to consider themselves as only "observant" or "modern Jews."

After his military service, Sender Goldreich began his studies at the Yeshiva but felt more drawn to commerce. As a young businessman, he stopped growing his beard and side locks. The practical aspect of hard work did not leave much time to study the Torah. In addition, Sender and "modern Jews" like him wanted to create a new Jewish image: Jews who successfully worked the land and were productive in business; Jews who were integrated into the country's life; Jews who moved forward to harness the possibilities emerging in the new world.

Sender became active in the wood trade. The entire region was densely wooded, and provided an inexhaustible source of lumber. He recognized the potential, and opened one of the town's largest logging firms, with the wood used to make paper for print shops. He focused mainly on getting contracts for cutting, selling and delivering wood to all areas in Poland, Galicia and Ukraine.

Due to his success in business and his leadership qualities, Sender slowly achieved a central, prominent position in town. Sender was good at making friends and was very popular among his peers. He employed local laborers in his lumber business, served on the local Jewish council and was active as an arbitrator in cases of commercial and personal disputes among the members of the community. Sender became a well-to-do, respected wood merchant and a leader of the Jewish community.

Sender was in his early thirties, a relatively late age by the Jewish standards of that time, when he married Elza Erdman. Her father was Sender's colleague in the lumber business and Elza was a lovely, pious woman with a generous heart.

Rabbi Shlomo Erdman, Yona's maternal grandfather, was one of the richest and most generous Jews in his town. His family tree went back to the Baal Shem Tov, Rabbi Israel Ben Eliezer, one of the founders of the Chassidic movement. Shlomo and his wife, Nudel, lived in the town of Yoshonka, where they raised ten children – five sons and five daughters, including Elza.

In addition to the lumber business, Erdman's enterprises included a cowshed with dozens of cows, a small dairy specializing in cheese, and another factory producing fertilizers from cow dung. Shlomo and Nudel's house was open to all, and they were always generous with the poor and whoever found themselves in difficult circumstances. People would say fondly that Shlomo and Nudel Erdman kept the herd of cows only to be able to provide milk to people in need.

Both the Goldreich and the Erdman families were good at combining their business and their social skills; whether in farming and working the land, or in business and trade. Almost every village in the area had its "representative" of the family. Their talents and connections earned them a prominent position in the entire district. Down-to-earth and rooted in the soil, strongly connected and loyal to each other, they created a splendid Jewish branch in the heart of Eastern Europe.

Following their wedding, Sender and Elza, bought a large house in the center of Turka. Sender and Elza's first son, Yitzhak (Eizo), was born in 1925. Yona was born in 1927 and Avraham (Bumek) was born in 1930. Sender and Elza provided their three children with a warm and loving home, a serene and pastoral childhood.

Yona fondly remembers a childhood surrounded by a large, close-knit family that included twenty aunts and uncles, and forty or fifty cousins, of whom fourteen lived close by in Turka. Yona remembers a lot of action.

The Goldreich family enjoyed all the trappings of "high society" at the time. Their house was built on the edge of the river, where they bathed in the summer. On hot days, the family used to enjoy each other's company during meals on the large veranda that surrounded the front of the house, while the children played their games. The house was lit by electricity produced by generators, unlike most houses that still used candles or gaslights. The restroom, located outdoors, was emptied directly into the river which served as a natural sewer (from which local residents of the rural area also pumped their water).

The Goldreich family had a "car and their own driver," meaning a horse and carriage with a coachman. There were two housemaids, one Jewish and the other Ukrainian, who did the housework. The Goldreichs had preferred seats at the synagogue, and their own cow provided milk for the children. Yona remembers how, as a five-year-old boy, he would accompany the maid to help her milk the cow. "Since nobody knew how to pasteurize milk back then, the maid would boil it, let it cool down and store it in the cellar, which was used as a refrigerator. We also stored meat there, in addition to sour cream and cheese made by my mother. Two strong gentiles were responsible for supplying the house with water. Every couple of days they would carry water in heavy barrels up from the river and the maid would boil it in a large cauldron. Only after it cooled down were we able to drink from it."

In contrast to the difficulty of making a living that affected many Jews in Turka, Yona remembers a childhood of plenty, without worries, in a shtetl (a Jewish neighborhood) where everyone knew one another. "We raised pigeons and adopted a dog named Rex," says Yona. "In the stable, there were horses that pulled the carriage when we traveled out of town to visit family or went on winter skiing vacations on the slopes of the snow-covered Carpathian Mountains."

A great mix of languages was heard in the house. Elza was an educated woman who read a lot and spoke many languages. From her, Yona learned Hebrew, Yiddish, German, Polish and Russian. "She was a good wife and a devoted mother. Everyone in Turka knew and respected her."

Elza was more observant than Sender. She kept a strict kosher kitchen. The Christian maid never cooked, the kitchen was run only by the Jewish maid, and meat and dairy were meticulously kept apart. "If one of the children ate cheese in the morning," Yona recounts, "he had to wait for six hours until he could have meat. Before Sabbath came, my mother would put the food in the oven for the entire night, and on Sabbath at noon, we were served a hot meal." Like all Jewish women in Turka, Elza adhered to the rules of modesty and wore long dresses. During the freezing winter days, she would wear a long fur coat, which gave her a feminine, elegant appearance.

In the summer, Elza would take Yona to the nearby fields and groves, sit under a tree and read him a book. She also gave the same personal attention to Eizo and Bumek. When Yona grew up and preferred playing soccer to going on an excursion with his mother, Elza would plead with him, "Yona'leh, come with me to the mountains." Yona cherishes the memory of those beautiful moments with his mother. Surrounded by nature and far from the clamor of home, Yona flew on the wings of imagination to far-away places as his mother, in her beloved, soft voice, told him wonderful stories.

Yona also recalls magical summer vacations when he, his brothers and their cousins would climb into a carriage and travel happily to one of their grandfathers' estates, riding for two and a half hours in each direction. "Sometimes," Yona remembers, "we would go up the mountain and walk all day long until we reached our grandfather's home."

Sometimes the brothers would spend the vacation at their Grandfather Shraga's farm in Botelka, and other times they were with Grandfather Shlomo in Yoshonka. Yona remembers heaven on earth: a natural paradise surrounded by forests, with flourmills and herds of cows and goats grazing on expansive meadows. There, the children would ride horses, milk cows, and roam the land, having fun in the wide open space, far away from the crowded town and its narrow streets. The little guests would spend the night in the barn, all of them together on the hay, near the cowshed. "How we loved sleeping there," Yona recounts. "At home, one had to obey rules and be clean and tidy; in the barn, though, we could run wild until late at night when we fell asleep, exhausted. Those were happy days, filled with fun and lots of laughter."

At grandfather Erdman's estate, which was very affluent, there was a big attraction at the time – a telephone. Yona remembers the silence that fell over the entire house whenever the phone rang. All the children would gather to watch in wonder: Grandfather was speaking on the telephone, and someone was listening to him in a faraway place!

Yona remembers the newspaper would arrive once a week. And, in the entire district, there were only two cars, "One belonged to the Mayor and the other one to the richest Jew." The town had one gas station, three radio receivers – one of them in the Goldreich family home – three physicians and three lawyers, all Jewish.

Every Friday, the town's many poor Jews stood in a long line in front of the Goldreich family home to receive Challah. Yona returned from school one Friday, when he was about ten years old, and there was the usual line of people waiting in front of his home. Yona heard a few muttering to themselves, "This one and that one have enough money… they could afford to buy Challah…"

"Dad," Yona approached his father, "this one does not need bread. Why do we give it to him?"

Yona's father imparted an important lesson to his son, "Do you see twenty people here? Thirty? If only one of them is in need of bread and we don't know who he is, we have to give bread to all of them. If God has blessed us, we are obliged to give to those who are not as fortunate as we are."

Indeed, Yona's parents put their values into action. Elza was part of the local Jewish charity organization and adopted the town orphanage. Sender gave alms in secret. His parents' values still resonate deeply with Yona.

Just as Yona learned the value of giving from his father, Sender had learned the importance of it from his own father. In the village of Botelka, where Shraga Fattal lived, there were only a few Jewish families. Since there was no synagogue, prayers were held on the Goldreich estate. To make sure there were enough Jewish men for the minyan, the quorum of ten needed for prayer, every Friday Shraga would invite poor people to spend the Sabbath with him. He would send his coachman to pick them up before the beginning of the Sabbath. On Sabbath Eve, they would dine at his table and sleep in the barn. The following day, they would pray with him. On Sunday, the coachman would take them home again. Yona recounts laughingly, "When a poor person was asked, 'How was the food at the Goldriech's?' he would answer, 'They gave us so much Challah bread to eat that when the meat and the fish were served, I couldn't eat any more.'"

All week long Jews in Turka waited for the weekend and, starting on Thursdays, a special atmosphere descended up on the town. In Poland, a country with a very cold climate, there were no showers with running water. Therefore, the Jews in

Turka used to bathe once a week. The women went to the mikvah, the ritual bath, on Thursday nights, and the men went there on Friday afternoons.

On Thursdays, when their mother went to the mikvah, Yona and his brothers enjoyed a special treat, which was considered a luxury at the time – a joint bath given to them by the maid. "She heated water on the oven, which was fueled by wood, poured buckets of hot water into the large bathtub and immersed us in it. She would scrub us with soap, shampoo our hair, rinse us one after the other and wrap us in thick, rough towels."

On Fridays, holding his mother's hand, little Yona used to accompany her to shop for the Sabbath. "Eating habits at the time were not like those of today," he remembers. "When we bought meat from the neighborhood butcher and he was cautious with the fat, people would complain, 'That cheater sold us meat without fat.' But the food was fresh. After the shochet (Jewish slaughterer) said the blessing, as was the custom, he would slaughter the chickens right before our eyes."

Every Friday afternoon, a few hours before the beginning of the Sabbath, the boys and their father would walk to the mikvah for the tvila, ritual immersion. It is one of Yona's best childhood memories. He remembers clearly the scalding water, the blows of the birch branches, which help the fragrant soap be absorbed by the skin, until it became red and hot. And then the dip into the refreshing cold water, cooling off, and the feeling of utter cleanliness as he put on the freshly laundered, good clothes for Sabbath.

On the Sabbath Eve, Turka became quiet and festive. Every family would walk to attend evening prayers in one of the town's five synagogues, each representing a different school of Judaism. Yona accompanied his father to the Sephardic Chassidic synagogue, belonging to the Chortkov community at whose Yeshiva Sender had studied in his youth. His mother, however, preferred to pray in the women's section of the Ashkenazi synagogue of the Sadiger community.* The next day, Yona and all the children waited impatiently for the Yizkor prayers, when they were "released" from the sanctuary and gathered to play in the front yard of the synagogue.

On the Sabbath, families visited with each other, eating, drinking, and enjoying each other's company. The children played together. During the summer, they swam in the river, boys and girls separately, of course.

Yona longingly remembers the weekends they used to spend with his maternal grandfather, Shlomo Erdman: starting with the Sabbath dinner, accompanied by songs and Chassidic melodies, up to the moving Havdalah ceremony marking the end of the Sabbath, after which his industrious grandfather hurried to get back to work.

༄

At the age of three, Yona started his primary education. As was the custom at the time, and like his father and grandfather before, as soon as he was out of his diapers, Yona was taken to the Cheder or Jewish primary school. No one was more delighted than Yona's parents on his first day at the Cheder. It was celebrated as a day of joy, a day of Mitzvah, on which a boy begins to study the Torah.*

Every day, Yona spent six hours in the company of twenty other small children his age. They learned texts from the Torah, as well as prayers and their tunes. He studied the stories of Moses, of Jacob the patriarch, and the commentaries of Rashi, the famous Jewish scholar, as well as excerpts from the Talmud.

---

* In Turka there were additional synagogues under the leadership of the Rabbi of Belz and the Rabbi of Sambor, in addition to the synagogue of the famous Chelm community, from the stories of Sholem Aleichem, author of "Fiddler on the Roof."

* The Jewish girls remained at home to help with housework and were taught Bible stories by private teachers.

Yona also learned some math and good manners, all under the guidance of a strict teacher. Discipline was severe at the Cheder. Those who were caught not concentrating or listening were punished by blows with a soft cane ("kanchik") on the palms of their hands.

From time to time, Yona was struck by mischievousness and slipped out of the classroom with his friends to play soccer on a deserted plot of land. When his father found out about this, Sender would pull down Yona's pants and give him a light spanking.

Sender considered himself to be a liberal Jew and believed that a Jewish upbringing had to be combined with a general education. "My father didn't buy a car, although he could afford it, because he believed education to be more important than luxury. He used to read us books, ensured that we spoke Hebrew, Yiddish and Polish and above all, that we studied mathematics, algebra and geometry." Therefore, Yona transferred to public school at the age of seven, and went to the Cheder in the afternoon hours and on Sundays. Sender also wanted to add a taste of Zionism to his children's education. Yona fell in love with stories about the Land of Israel which his mother read to him and his brothers. He would laugh until he cried when his parents took him to watch the performances of Jewish plays that were staged at the local theater.*

When Yona transferred to the regular school, he would play with his Jewish friends after school and hardly had any contact with non-Jewish children. Christian children used to start working at the age of seven or eight. Only a few of them went to school, unlike most of the Jewish children who were educated, since the Jews considered knowledge and education the two most important values. "At school, the Jewish children used to

---

* The starring actors were famous comedians Shimon Divan and Israel Schumacher who brought the stories of Sholes Aleichem to the stage. They spoke Yiddish and coined the saying, "Laughter is good for the health."

get better grades, after already having four years of schooling at the Cheder," says Yona. "We knew how to read, write and do our numbers better than the gentile children. When the Jewish students received good grades, they would accuse us of cheating. In those days, there was no television and there were few distractions. We didn't have much to do, so we sat and studied."

Yona was considered a good student. He excelled in the sciences, and loved to play chess during recess. He inherited his love for books from his mother, and read them eagerly: political and philosophical works, books on general and Jewish history. Thus, he acquired a broad general education.

If life would have run its usual course, Yona, like his older brother, Eizo, and most of the well-to-do Jewish children, would have attended the Gymnasia. But fate had something else in store for him.

☙

The Treaty of Versailles and its promises were one thing, reality was another. The political and economic success of the Jews increased anti-Semitism. The press attacked the "covenant" (according to which the Polish government had agreed to respect the religious and social rights of the Jews), and accused the Jews of collaboration with the Germans. Anti-Semitism was again expressed openly. It was deeply ingrained in both the Catholic citizens who did not like that the "murderers of Jesus" were gaining a foothold in the villages, and the rulers, who considered the Jews a weak and defenseless minority,

Private initiatives stopped, and the Jews were pushed out of their traditional occupations. The sewing workshops in Turka, which employed hundreds of Jews, were scaled down or closed, and many workers were laid off. As a consequence, the social gap grew. Only a few were very rich; most joined the ranks of the poor and became destitute peddlers. In those days, there was a well-known saying in Turka, that anyone who had enough flour on Thursday to bake the Challah (bread for Sabbath), was lucky indeed.

When hopes for a Jewish Autonomy in Eastern Europe diminished, the Jews woke up to a new dream, the Zionist dream: The establishment of a Jewish national home in the Land of Israel. Turka was swept by the new wave and turned into a lively Jewish and Zionist center. Hebrew language courses were opened. HaShomer Hatza'ir, a Jewish youth movement, paraded in the streets, singing about settling and farming in the Land of Israel. The birthdays of the Zionist visionary Theodor Herzl and of the Hebrew poet Haim Nachman Bialik were openly celebrated with parties and special events. Abba Chushi (originally Schneller), a native of Turka who eventually became the mayor of Haifa, had worked for Sender Goldreich in his youth before leaving for Palestine as a pioneer. Now, he returned to his hometown to convince Jews to follow him to the Land of Israel; as a result, a number of young people left their families and went to Palestine.

In the evenings, Zionist meetings were held, and discussions of current Jewish-Zionist issues took place. Opposing Zionism was the Agudat Israel organization, led by the Rabbi of Gur, to which most of Poland's orthodox Jews belonged. They were satisfied with their religious and cultural autonomy, and rejected the Zionist idea. They were waiting for the Messiah, and claimed that upon his arrival, he would lead them to the Promised Land.

Sender was fascinated by the Zionist idea. As someone who was raised on the Bible's stories, he envisioned the Jews walking in the footsteps of the Holy Scriptures' heroes, reviving their vision of inheriting the Promised Land. Sender was among the founders and supporters of the Akiva movement in Turka, which encouraged the younger generation to study agriculture, so they would be able to work the land in the state of Israel once it was established.

Across the border, in Germany, a new leader rose to power – Adolf Hitler. The winds of war and hatred of the Jews started blowing across Europe. Poland again fell into a deep economic depression and, as usual, the Jews were blamed. Fear of the powerful German neighbor grew. Hostility against the Jews intensified, as did the number of attacks and boycotts throughout Poland.

At the end of the 1930s, the anti-Semitic parties in Poland established commando units, similar to those of the Nazis, which incited pogroms and demanded the expulsion of Jews from Poland. Even the socialists, who initially rejected anti-Semitism, started to claim that only Jews willing to assimilate into the country's population could remain in Poland.

Sender and his friends would often sit in coffee houses and discuss politics. Yona, who loved cakes and sweets, would join his father for these meetings and learned how serious the situation was. Everyone worried about the worsening economic situation and the rise of Hitler in Germany. They spoke of the Land of Israel, Palestine, as a new hope and about new immigration options opening up for Jews. Quite a few heated arguments erupted around the coffee house tables. Baron Edmond de Rothschild called for Jews to immigrate to the Land of Israel. Baron Morris Hirsch addressed those who would not consider this option and waited for the Messiah, encouraging them to settle in Argentina.

Success stories of Jews who had left Poland fascinated those who stayed. Excited, Elza read letters she received from family members from Galicia who became successful furriers in Paris, and from other family members who opened a real estate agency in London. Enchanted for hours, she looked at photographs from relatives who had left for the United States, They smiled happily and stood in front of a big car, unlike any ever seen in Turka.

The majority of Jews in town who adhered to modern Judaism started to realize they should immigrate to the Land of Israel. Sender, who was an active Zionist in the HaPoel HaMizrahi movement, considered leaving Poland. "If we could sell the house and the business, we would be able to go to Palestine or Argentina," Yona heard his father whisper to his mother.

As a counterpoint to Zionism, a new ideology of Communism arrived from across the border and took a strong hold among Turka's Jews. Jewish youngsters were taken by the idea of absolute equality, believing this would be their salvation. This phenomenon caused strife and split quite a few families apart, including Yona's family. Wealthy Uncle Moshe Hirth was astonished to find out that his daughter had joined the "Reds." And Kaman Meiner, Elza's uncle, was appointed secretary of the Communist Party in Turka. He fulfilled this position clandestinely until he was caught and put into prison.

The first family member to be affected by the deteriorating economic situation was Uncle Shlomo whose license to sell alcohol was revoked. He understood there was no future in Turka and smuggled his daughter, with the help of hefty bribes, to Western Europe where she completed her medical studies.

Sender also experienced a decline in business. When the owner of the local movie theater proposed using the wall of Sender's house to hang movie posters in exchange for watching those movies for free, Sender saw an opportunity to provide his family with some entertainment during difficult times.

The lines of people in front of the Goldreich house who came to receive charity and bread on Fridays grew even larger. Many of those people were starving. People sold simple items, clothes and shoes, to get food for their children. Almost every day Elza invited hungry families, unemployed and destitute, to join their dinner table.

Every bit of information about what was happening in Germany and of Hitler's intentions was analyzed with increasing worry. The more their parents tried to hide their concerns from the children, the more Yona and his brothers couldn't help but notice the lack of certainty on their parents' faces. The radio broadcast warnings of a German attack and encouraged the people of Turka to prepare shelters. The Polish military appeared in town and started recruiting young men. The tension was palpable.

Then came the terrible news – surprising, even though it had been anticipated. On September 1, 1939, World War II started. Adolf Hitler marked the first target of the Reich's army – Poland.

No sirens sounded. Without any warning, German aircraft dove towards town, one after the other. Turka had never before experienced an aerial attack. The noise was tremendous. The residents, screaming with terror, tried to find shelter from the bombs. The railway, the train station and the adjacent bridge, Turka's only connections to the outside world, were bombed and completely destroyed. The town was cut off.

Yona and his brothers were terrified. Until now, they had felt safe and protected. They had trusted their parents would protect them from all evil – but bombs were falling from the sky, and there was no shelter. Even Elza's embrace could not help, neither could Sender's strong shoulders.

The shining fighter planes with the Reich's swastikas maneuvered through the skies above the city. The bombing of Turka continued for several minutes. It seemed like an eternity before the planes turned and disappeared beyond the horizon.

A deadly silence fell over the town. Residents fearfully peeked out from their doors. Everyone was in shock. Women cried, men bit their lips nervously. The children had never seen their parents like this.

Yona was just twelve years old when World War II erupted in his own backyard.

1920, Turka: Elza Goldreich

1932, Turka: Yona's parents, Elza and Sender Goldreich, in better days

1932: Grandfather Shlomo Erdman

1937: Summer vacation at Botelka Village where Grandfather Fatel Goldreich lived. R-L Uncle Shmuel, Aunt Pesia, two friends, and Fishel with brother Izio at 12

CHAPTER TWO

On September 1, 1939, without any declaration of war, Nazi Germany invaded Poland from the west, occupied it within about two weeks and ended its existence as an independent country. About two weeks later, the Red Army started moving east from Russia into the Ukrainian region that had been under Polish control. Turka was delivered into the hands of the Soviets in the wake of a "dirty," secret pact between Stalin and Hitler. The agreement determined that Poland would be divided between Russia and Germany. The secret pact violated all the settlements world leaders had agreed upon after World War I.*

A young woman appeared at the door of the Goldreich family's home. She was a Jewish teacher captivated by the lure of Communism. She "proposed" that Elza fly a red flag, "like all the houses in town." This, she said, would be a sign of welcome for the Russians' arrival. Not having much of a

---

* The Molotov-Ribbentrop Pact was signed on August 23, 1939, between Stalin and Hitler, behind the back of Poland. According to the pact, named after the foreign ministers of the two countries – German's foreign minister, Joachim von Ribbentrop, and Soviet Russia's foreign minister, Vyacheslav Molotov – Germany and Russia agreed not to attack each other for a period of ten years.

choice, Elza took a piece of red cloth and put it up in front of the house.

Turka was taken by the Russians without a shot. The small number of Polish soldiers who were stationed in the city surrendered on the spot, and were taken as prisoners of war. The hundreds of Communists in town received the Russian commissars with open arms, as heroes.

About ten percent of Turka's Jews were completely secular. They had distanced themselves from belonging to the Jewish faith, advocating atheism and doubting the existence of God. They were looking for a worldly solution, and therefore were easily captivated by the charms of Communism, which promised to turn the world around, bringing equality for all.

"And since most of Turka's Jews were poor, it was only natural that they became attracted to the ideas of Communism," explains Yona. "In their dreams, with the Communists everyone would be equal. They would all have a roof over their heads and food to eat. From their point of view, that alone already meant a lot."

It was not surprising that Turka's Jews were among the leaders of the Communist Party in town. The admiration for Communism was, above all, driven by the thought that it would end anti-Semitism, by far the greatest trouble afflicting Eastern European Jews. "In part, this way of thinking was right," says Yona. "The Jews were a significant force in the Russian Revolution, and even one of the initiators of the Communist Revolution, Leon Trotsky, was a Jew."

After the death of Vladimir Ilich Lenin, the leader of the Communist Revolution, the Jewish Communists hoped that Trotsky, the son of a Ukrainian Jewish peasant would become his successor. However, in 1922, Joseph Stalin, ("Stalin" means "steel" in Russian) a former Christian seminary student from Georgia prevailed over Trotsky.*

The new rulers in Turka started operating without delay. The former local leadership and those who were declared "enemies of the people" by the Communists were arrested, and some were executed. The Communists in Turka joyfully joined the "Russian liberators" and were conscripted in order to implement the Revolution swiftly. The Jewish Communist Party even announced a celebration for the Red Army soldiers.

Among the first appointments made by the Communists was the post of mayor. Yona's uncle, Kalman Meiner, who had spent years in prison for his affiliation with Communism, was chosen. However, this did nothing to help the rest of the family's members.

Within days, Turka was painted red, the color of the revolution. Without delay, the confiscations started. The Jewish Communists provided lists of the rich Jews, the bourgeoisie. The commissars were quick to confiscate shops and factories, to take control of all food and clothing resources, and redistribute them according to the new values. The lumber business owned by Sender was confiscated.

Yona's father was not a Communist, but he didn't dare stand up against the new rulers. The red fabric, which continued to flutter in front of his house, was of no help. Goldreich's family wealth turned them into bourgeoisie. According to the Communism principles, the assets of the bourgeoisie were taken away and "distributed among the people," while they were sentenced to be re-educated by hard labor in the snow-covered wilderness of Siberia.

---

* Following Stalin's rise to power, the new leader persecuted Trotsky. Fearing for his life, he fled to Mexico and was assassinated there by Stalin's henchmen, The KGB, in 1935.

The crowd of people lining up on Fridays to receive their Challah for the Sabbath from Elza disappeared. Now food was handed out by the Communists, with the entire population receiving "equal portions." The abundance vanished from the Goldreich household, and the future became overshadowed by uncertainty.

The Goldreichs found it difficult to get used to the new laws. "Under Communism, everyone was indeed equal," Yona explains with his own special sense of humor, "but they were equal in poverty. Truth be told, people are not equal, that is impossible. But the Communists proved that if everyone is made poor, it is possible to make everyone the same."

༺ ༻

The Russians arrival in Turka turned the safe and peaceful world of twelve-year-old Yona upside down. The first wealthy house to be plundered was that of his Uncle Moshe Hirth, who managed to escape beforehand while leaving all his assets and possessions behind. There was no one in the house when the new mayor, Uncle Kalman, took over and declared it the new "City Hall."

The second building to be confiscated in the name of the revolution was the Goldreich family home.

At first, Sender, like other owners of large houses, was ordered to "lodge" the homeless. Overnight, the Goldreich home was filled with the rattle of the poor families who moved in.

Elza tried her very best to maintain a daily routine, as if everything was as it should be. The children were sent to school and studied Judaism in the afternoons. Yet, all schools, including those attended by Yona and his brother, underwent a fast Stalinist brainwash. The children had to memorize the Communist propaganda, and the curriculum was altered accordingly. The classroom walls were covered with Communist slogans, and every day began with the students "praying" for the safety of Stalin, "Sun of the Nations."

The Communists erased any remnant, custom and way of life that resembled a ritual of religion or faith. This harsh attitude affected everyone: Christians, both Catholics and Protestants, and, of course, Jews. "Christians were forbidden to attend churches and Jews were forbidden to pray in synagogues," says Yona. "The toughest verdict was having to go to school on Saturdays, the Jewish holy day of rest. If you didn't show up at school on Saturday, your parents would be punished." In the beginning, the Russians made it obligatory also to attend school on Sundays, the Christian day of rest, and randomly chose another day of the week as a day off. The decree didn't hold for long, and in the end, the Communists settled on Sunday as the official and only day of rest; the Jews were still obliged to attend school every Saturday. The Communists did not approve of religious studies and prayers, which the Jewish children attended in the afternoon. Nevertheless, they dared not abolish the synagogues and Cheder (the Jewish primary school) yet. That would come later.

A law was issued forbidding Jews to keep domesticated animals. Fortunately, Sender had already transferred the family cow from the house and "stored" it in his coachman's house.

The members of the Goldreich family tried to follow the new path and not get into trouble with the new rulers, yet there was one thing they would not give up: listening to Western radio broadcasts. These programs gave them their only hope, even though listening to a foreign station was considered a serious offense. "We had no choice," says Yona. "The Russian radio stations were broadcasting propaganda and lies. The Communists, of course, didn't want us to know what was going on in the world. So my dad hid the radio and together we would listen quietly and secretly to news from the world."

On the one hand, the Communists gradually took over every aspect of life in Turka. On the other hand, Turka's population became increasingly carried away with the "revolution," and soldiers of the Red Army were the city's most eligible bachelors.

Sender and Elza knew exactly what to expect for being "rich bourgeoisie" – twenty Jewish families of the same status had already been "chosen" and put on trains that took them to one of the labor camps in Siberia. Once there, they would undergo a "re-education program" while being engaged in long hours of hard labor, day after day, in one of the coldest places on earth. Many never returned from there. A number of the Goldreich family members, four uncles and two aunts, who attempted to leave the Polish territories occupied by the Germans and cross over to the Russian side, were caught by the Communists, labeled as "rich," and deported to Siberia to work in the coal mines.

Keeping a low profile, Elza began preparing everything for their impending deportation. She knitted knapsacks and packed them with necessary items.

"I made a deal with the commissar," said Sender one afternoon. He spoke in a quiet voice, as though sharing a secret. "We are not being sent to Siberia, but we have to leave the house." The news actually calmed Elza and the children a little.

"We were almost ready to leave for Siberia on the next train. There was great joy and relief that we were not sent to that hellhole," recounts Yona. "Although we were forced to leave our home, we did not have to leave Turka. This event has taught me that a person can never know what the future entails for him. What seems to be good turns out to be bad, and vice versa. At the time, when my uncles were sent to Siberia, it seemed they had been struck by bad luck. However, ironically, the fact that they were deported to Siberia kept them alive and saved them from the Holocaust. I often wonder what would have happened if my father had not succeeded in closing a 'deal' with the Communist politicians."

Yona remembers every minute of that winter day in late 1939 when the Goldreich family was thrown out of their home. The Red Army soldiers, policemen in uniform and the Communist officials appeared at the door. "The time has come," the commander informed them, looking Sender in the eye to remind him of the deal. The family had to leave within an hour.

The invaders quickly went through all the rooms and plundered everything that took their fancy. Yona and his family hastily packed a few suitcases with clothes that had already been prepared by Elza. The Communists urged them to get it over with quickly. "Out! Out!" they shouted. A few minutes later, their own door was slammed behind the family.

The Goldreich family picked up their meager belongings and turned their backs on the only home Yona had ever known. "All we took with us were a few suitcases in which my mom had hidden some gold jewelry, chains and diamonds," explains Yona. "In those days, especially in times of war, people preferred not to keep money, because they never knew how much it would be worth. When the Germans invaded Poland, the Polish currency, the Zloty, lost its value overnight. Consequently, anybody who had a little wealth would buy gold, jewelry and diamonds, and according to the amount of jewelry people had, they would evaluate their wealth."

Heads hanging low and hearts full of worry, the Goldreichs walked to their driver's house. Sender's Jewish coachman was a poor man but he had a generous heart. He let the Goldreichs rent a room in his modest house. Yona's parents slept on the only bed. Eizo, Yona and Bumek slept on the floor, bundled up together. It was a small space but they had each other.

Living conditions were difficult. "My mother, dedicated and efficient as always, attempted to preserve the family structure and the children's education," recounts Yona. "Before, she had two maids, and now she was doing everything herself, but she never complained. The situation was much worse for many Jews in the city."

A few days later, Yona returned to see what had become of their home. He discovered the Communists had made the house the premises of the Turka Fire Brigade.

News about the fate of other family members reached the crowded room. His parents were no longer able to speak in private so Yona heard how the Communists had confiscated the farming estates of his paternal grandfather, Shraga Fattal, in Botelka, and of his maternal grandfather, Shlomo Erdman, in Yoshonka. "Everything was transferred to the 'People's Government,' the houses, the property, my Grandfather Shlomo's herds and my Grandfather Shraga's warehouses," says Yona.

Sender was a smart businessman and started trading on the black market. He saw what the Russians lacked – clothing and shoes – and sold to them under the table. Thanks to his connections, Sender was allowed to partially renew his lumber business, provided that he agreed to only work with the authorities. "Luckily, we always had food because of my father, and the cow he was smart enough to keep," says Yona. "The most important thing in those days and later on, as the war continued, was food. With my very own eyes I saw my schoolmates become walking skeletons." Although the Goldreichs were in a dire situation, Yona's parents shared what little they had and secretly sent preserved food to Sender's brothers and sisters who had been deported to Siberia, and wrote that they suffered from severe hunger.

There were quite a few Jews in Turka who profited from the Communist occupation, either through the posts to which they were appointed, the property they now controlled, or because of new economic possibilities. Uncle Mordechai Erdman, for instance, expanded his bakery after he managed to get a contract to supply bread to the Red Army. Erdman, who was the father of six, was able to get this contract thanks to his eldest son,* who was among the Jewish Communist leaders in Turka and had contacts in the new regime. For Yona and his brothers, this meant they got to have baked good from time to time.

The stronger the Communists' grip on Turka, the safer the Communists felt to go after the orthodox Jews. They started to shut down synagogues (and, at the same time, Christian churches). Gangs of Soviet commissars and local Ukrainians robbed and plundered the synagogues. Torah scrolls and ritual objects disappeared. Rabbis and believers tried their best to hide what they could, whether it was a Torah scroll or a parochet (curtain of the Holy Ark). But most of the synagogues' contents were destroyed. The buildings were confiscated and converted for public use. This was also the end of the Cheder in Turka. With the attempts of the new regime to erase any remnants of faith, the old world slowly disappeared.

A strict prohibition on carrying out religious rituals – circumcisions, Bar Mitzvahs and weddings – was imposed. Registering a birth or a marriage could be done only through civil procedures. However, Turka's Jews kept their tradition alive in secret. Jewish weddings continued to take place underground, not always in the presence of a rabbi. Circumcisions and Bar Mitzvahs were held in hidden places, without the traditional Torah reading in the synagogue. Prayers on the Sabbath Eve were whispered in sealed rooms or cellars. The places where prayers were to take place were conveyed by word of mouth and kept strictly secret.

"The Jewish life was led secretly," recounts Yona. "Father used to put on his tefillin (phylacteries), while making sure that no one would see him. And mother, despite the difficulty,

---

* This son later lived in Russia and then immigrated to Israel, where he became a Socialist.

continued to keep Kosher. On Fridays, we would take the chicken to the shochet (the Jewish slaughterer) and pay him. He would say the blessing and slaughter it in hiding."

In September 1940, the time came for Yona's Bar Mitzvah. Under different circumstances, Elza and Sender would have announced the event well ahead of time, and prepared a huge celebration for the entire family, who would have arrived from all over the district. It should have been the happiest day of his life. On the day of his Bar Mitzvah, Yona would have proudly stepped onto the synagogue's stage and read the week's chapter from the Torah. Candy would have been thrown by everyone in attendance. Blessings would have been issued all over the synagogue, reverberating from one end to the other. This would have been followed by a meal of royal proportions, accompanied by the sounds of a Klezmer band playing Jewish tunes. Above all, the Bar Mitzvah boy would have eagerly looked forward to the many presents he was about to receive from the guests.

Such a Bar Mitzvah celebration could not take place. Therefore, the date of Yona's Bar Mitzvah was kept secret and told to no one. Preparations for Yona's big day were carried out underground. Yona secretly studied and memorized the words of his Torah section in Hebrew.

On the day of the Bar Mitzvah, early in the morning, Yona and his father hurried along the narrow streets of Turka towards the Rabbi's house. They tried not to arouse suspicion and made sure that no one followed them. The Rabbi nervously waited. The windows in his room had already been carefully covered. Unwanted eyes would not be able to witness the "crime" about to occur inside.

Sender took out his tefillin and instructed his son. For the first time in his life, Yona was required to fulfill the commandment incumbent on every male Jew, every day. Yona's father first wrapped the hand tefillin around his son's arm and taught him that the tefillin box is put on pointing towards the heart. After that, Sender placed the head tefillin on Yona's head, above the forehead. Finally, he showed his son how to create, with the leather strap, the form of the Hebrew letter "shin" on his wrist and the back of his hand. Then he explained how this letter, combined with the knot tied behind his head in the form of the Hebrew letter "dalet," and the shape of the knot on the arm, which resembles the Hebrew letter "yod," spell "Shadai" (Almighty), one of God's names.

When the tefillin had been placed as required by Jewish law, Yona whispered, full of reverence: *"Baruch ata, Adonai, Elohenu, Melekh haolam, asher kidshanu bemitzvotav vetzivanu lehaniach tefillin."* (Praised be you, Lord, our God, who sanctified us with his commandments and ordered us to put on tefillin).

After he took off the tefillin's straps, Yona whispered the words of his Torah reading in Hebrew. His only listeners were his father and the Rabbi, who hurried him along with his eyes, out of fear that the forbidden ritual might be discovered.

Barely an hour later, Yona and his father were on their way back to the little room that served as their home. When they entered, Yona's brothers joyfully surrounded him. His mother, with tears in her eyes, blessed her son, "Now you have to maintain the Jewish faith even more."

No meal, no party, no musicians, no guests and no presents. It is one of the most significant events in the life of every Jewish boy, but Yona's Bar Mitzvah was celebrated behind closed doors, in utmost secrecy.

༺༻

On June 22, 1941, Hitler declared war on the Soviet Union. News of the Germans' swift advance along the entire Russian front spread like wildfire in Turka. Town after town, district after district fell into the hands of the Nazis. The Russians packed in a hurry. It was clear to everyone that within a few hours, or a few days at the most, life would be turned upside down again. Many Jews, who had had enough of the Russian regime, were glad to finally get rid of Communism. They assumed the German occupation would be good for the Jews.

CHAPTER THREE

The Nazis stormed Poland and quickly proceeded eastward toward Turka. The Communists ran for their lives, but not before brutally killing all their prisoners, who were mostly anti-Communists.

"The Russians retreated from Turka in panic, while calling upon the Jews to flee with them," Yona recounts. "About four hundred young Jews left with the Communists and enlisted in the Red Army."

Local Ukrainian militias took advantage of the governmental vacuum. During the few days between the departure of the Russians and the arrival of the Germans, Ukrainian residents of the Lvov region showed their true colors, and the hatred they harbored toward the Jews. Although the Jews provided work and livelihood, their success seemed to ignite envy and hatred. Anarchy reigned as the Ukrainians robbed the Jews, drove them out of their homes in the rural areas and forced many to flee to the cities without any possessions.

For the first time in his life, fourteen-year-old Yona experienced the terror of a pogrom. In Yoshonka, where his grandfather Rabbi Shlomo Erdman lived, the villagers didn't wait for the new rulers, and started massacring Jews. Rabbi

Erdman's house was robbed and destroyed by his own workers, the same workers for whom he had provided livelihood for many years. Yona's Uncle Hillel Erdman managed to escape into the woods that surrounded the village. Sadly, his wife did not escape the massacre. Yona's Aunt Margalit was one of the dozens of murder victims.

In an ironic paradox, when the Nazis arrived in the village a few days after the riot in Yoshonka, they were furious about the "pogrom." It was considered an unacceptable breach of public order. The Nazis announced that all Jewish property was to be returned to its owners. They tried to recover the loot and give it back to the Jews. Aunt Margalit and the others who were murdered could not be brought back.

"The day the Germans entered Turka, Thursday, July 1, 1941, is deeply etched in my memory," Yona recalls. "When we saw the Germans arrive in Turka we were glad, because we hoped we could return to our house. The first days were quiet, and the German commander stopped the attempts of the Ukrainian police to expand the pogroms."

The Goldreichs received an encouraging gesture. They were permitted to return to their home, although they were only allowed to occupy the upper floor. The ground floor remained at the disposal of the Ukrainian Fire Brigade. In the yard, Hungarian soldiers, who were incorporated into the Nazi forces, built a car repair shop under the command of a Hungarian officer from a noble family. A relationship developed between the commander of the mechanics unit and Sender Goldreich. At that time, the Hungarians were known for their fair attitude towards the Jews so the presence of the Hungarians led to a feeling of well-being.

The joy over the Communists' departure did not last long. Slowly, the Nazis' true face revealed itself.

The Nazis hurried to establish the Judenrat and the Jewish Police. At first, no one suspected their real purpose. The

Judenrat was the Jewish Council. It was responsible for implementation of the German policy towards the Jewish population. Its eight members were Turka's leading Jewish citizens. The head of the Jewish community, Joshua Nachman Meiner, was appointed director of the Judenrat. Yona's uncle, Joshua Erdman, became a member of the council.

The Jewish Police were assigned to enforce German policy. Its commander was Jacob Lev Broiner. On one hand, Broiner was known to be a good-hearted man, but he was also one of the most corrupt men in Turka's Jewish community. The Jewish policemen used to wear a purple hat and an armband with the inscription "Patrol – Jewish Police."

Yona's sixteen-and-a-half year-old brother, Eizo, was drafted into the Jewish Police and moved to their kserktin (camp). Eizo believed that he could protect his family in this position.

The Nazis demanded that the Judenrat confiscate any valuable objects from its Jewish brethren in order to support the German war effort. Food storerooms, which wealthy Jews had prepared for emergencies, were emptied for the benefit of the new rulers. The little property they had left was taken away. An order was issued that required Jews to wear a white ribbon with the Star of David painted on. That was the beginning of the Yellow Patch that Jews in all German-occupied areas were later forced to sew on their clothes. Those wearing the white ribbon, even a boy like Yona, were not allowed to venture even as far as across the street from their home. A man who looked "like a Jew" but not wearing a patch was ordered to pull his pants down and show his genitals. Anyone found to be circumcised was shot at once.

The German commander in town was replaced by a new one and the situation deteriorated even more. The new commander, Zelenka, was an alcoholic, and he ordered the Judenrat to supply him with liquor, which had become as valuable as gold. Whenever he did not receive his quota of alcohol, Zelenka would attack any Jew who happened to be in the vicinity.

The Germans took away the Jews' right to trade. Jewish shops were plundered by local Ukrainians and closed down. The few grocery shops, which had limited commodities to begin with, were forbidden to sell to Jews.

All schools were closed. Elza and Sender tried to pay for a few weekly hours of tutoring for Yona and Bumek, who had not finished their elementary school education. A teacher came to the family's house in secret and whispered the lessons in Hebrew. His fees were paid in food. When food became even scarcer, and there was barely enough to satisfy the basic needs of the family, there was no choice but to stop the lessons.

The German army started pressing Jews into forced labor. At first, they were paid a small sum. Later, when there was less and less food in town, the workers labored for a bit of food. The labor included repairing the railroad tracks damaged by German air attacks at the beginning of the war. They rebuilt a bridge the Russians had blown up during their retreat, and they paved roads for the German vehicles.

Everyone was recruited for the German war effort, even teenagers. Fourteen-year-old Yona was forced to work one day per week. "Most of the time, I was made to work with other teens, sweeping the streets at best, or in the worst case, carrying baskets filled with dirt to sites where the Germans were building," says Yona. But one day was especially difficult. "They drove us to the quarries near Turka. They gave me a heavy hammer and demanded that I pound rocks into gravel for ten consecutive working hours. I was lucky that I was only recruited to work there once. Others, who were forced to do such work every day, could not bear the strain, and did not survive the harsh winter."

Without trade and paying work, Turka's Jews, including the Goldreich family, gradually became impoverished.

Food became increasingly scarce. Food stamps, which the Germans distributed, had no value since it became impossible to obtain basic commodities. The collapse of agriculture in Europe was felt in each and every home in town. Famine fell upon Turka, and its first victims were the Jews. What little flour remained out of the reach of the Gendarmerie (the German civil police) was given to the forced laborers. Without bread, thousands of people slowly starved to death.

The Jewish soup kitchen had supplied a little food to five hundred hungry people every day. It was the last resort of the starving but closed down due to the lack of food and funds.

Hunger became a way of life in Turka. Most meals were based on potatoes. Yet even this staple food became costly and increasingly rare. Children wandered around in the streets, their bellies swollen from hunger. Women made meals out of virtually nothing to feed their families.

The menace of hunger did not pass over the Goldreich family. The portions Elza served the children became smaller every day. Progressively less food was available in their home. Although Yona did not actually feel hunger, he worried as food decreased. Elza did the impossible trying to put food on the table for her children. One day she acquired loaves of bread from the surplus of the German army. The loaves were green with mold. Elza added potato peelings and baked them again, turning the loaves into a "delicacy" that filled their stomachs for a night.

Getting food became the predominant, if not the exclusive, occupation of every Jew in Turka. "And if someone dared to go to a nearby field to steal a vegetable or a fruit, and was caught by the Nazis, they would kill him on the spot," Yona recalls with terror. "Two friends of mine from the Cheder, who were starving, crept into the field and stole some vegetables.

The Nazis walked them along the street, gun barrel in their backs. They could barely walk because of the hunger. They were facing the Jewish cemetery. A few minutes later, we heard some gunshots and the dying screams of those miserable souls."

Yona remembers that rich people, like the Goldreich's neighbor, Meir Reisser, subsisted on potato peelings. "There weren't too many ways to prepare potato peelings, and thus those who were 'lucky' ate the same thing every day. They would cook the potato peelings in salt water, add a few ground grains of oat and bake the mixture."

The poor, like Yona's friend David Trauber, the son of a stonecutter, ate a grass called "labadeh," which served as cattle fodder in ordinary times. A large quantity of the grass was collected, it was cooked in a huge laundry pot and then the mixture was made into "burgers." This food caused severe digestive problems, which sometimes led to death. Yona watched in pain as his childhood friend's belly swelled up because the grass was so hard to digest. Yona's friends were dying in front of his very eyes. "They looked like walking skeletons, dying. Their bellies blown up, their eyes sunken in their sockets, and their cheekbones and vertebrae sticking out," remembers Yona. "To this day, I am haunted by the horrific images of my starving friends."

The Goldreichs survived thanks to Sender's commercial talent, and his friendship with the Hungarian Commander of the mechanics stationed in their front yard. The Commander, the son of a noble family, bought gold and diamonds from Jews, and made the Goldreich family's house his home. With the Commander's assistance, Sender established a small black market for basic commodities smuggled from Hungary. Sender sold his merchandise to those who could still afford to buy. Since money no longer had value, the market was based on barter: food for clothing, jewelry, furniture, carpets, and other objects.

Before the onset of winter, economic hardships forced Sender to sell the family's cow, which had provided them with milk for years. He invested part of his earnings into tobacco, which was smuggled into Turka by Hungarian soldiers. Tobacco was the only permitted luxury substance and was nearly impossible to obtain. Those addicted to nicotine were prepared to pay almost any price for it. Sender recruited Yona and Bumek to package it.

It was the Hungarian Commander who first warned them of the fate awaiting Jews and it was far harsher than their current situation. Upon his return from a tour of the surrounding areas, the Commander told Sender about the disappearance of entire rural Jewish communities and about ghettos for Jews in the big cities. He reported that hundreds, if not thousands, of Jews were killed and buried in mass graves in the fields and forests surrounding the towns and villages.

The Hungarian officer urged Sender to leave Turka immediately, before it was too late. He offered to help with their escape. The idea was for the family to cross the border, hiding under the seats of a Hungarian military truck. On the other side, relatives of the helpful officer would take them in. Sender and Elza spent the entire night quietly discussing the situation. They were willing to give everything they had left in order to carry out the plan to escape.

Unfortunately, the hard winter of 1941-42 fell upon them, and thwarted their escape plan. Huddled under their blankets in the corner of the room, the children listened as their father promised their mother, "We will survive the winter and flee in the summer." They waited for that first ray of sunshine.

The Final Solution, initiated by Adolf Eichmann as a plan to annihilate all European Jews, was implemented gradually. "Hitler did not hide his ambition to 'clean' Europe of the Jews," says Yona. "First he wanted to drive them out and the world kept quiet. While the Jews in Germany believed his intentions were true and started escaping to France, Spain, England, Palestine and other countries, most of the Jews in Poland did not grasp the full extent of the danger. 'God will not allow Hitler to do the evil deed he conspires to do,' they said. Then Eichmann took another step, killing the Jews instead of driving them out. The first victims were children and old people since the Nazis could not use them for forced labor. Hitler still didn't dare to do the killing in Germany itself, for fear of public reaction. However, far from sight, in Poland, Czechoslovakia and Ukraine, the annihilation machine worked at its full capacity."

Jewish professionals were gathered by the gendarmes and deported to far-away labor camps. It was made clear to them that any attempt to evade, resist or escape would result in the death of the families they left behind. Most of them didn't resist, didn't escape and never came back.

One day, a nightly curfew was announced for all Jews, and they were forbidden to light lamps after sunset. A few days later, the curfew was extended to part of the day.

The winter took its toll every day. The snow never stopped falling. Temperatures dropped far below zero. It was freezing cold. One could only dream about firewood. Then the Germans, freezing themselves, imposed another prohibition on the Jews: It was forbidden to own or wear furs. The Jewish police collected all fur clothing and blankets from Jewish houses and "donated" them to the German army. Elza had to give up her favorite fur coat, a cherished gift from her husband.

Every morning, the hearse from the Jewish cemetery drove through town and collected the dead Jews from their homes and off the streets. Neighbors, family members and Yona's friends from his days in the Cheder died one after the other. The terrible famine was the main cause of death in Turka, but the freezing cold also took its toll. Yona recalls at least five funerals per day.

The Nazi secret police, the Gestapo, were infamous for their cruelty. During the winter they came to Turka. Led by their commander, Madrohovich, members of the Gestapo took pride in wearing their symbol – the skull and crossbones. The Gestapo's task was to implement the genocide of the Jews.

The first order was to vacate thirty furnished rooms in Jewish houses for the Gestapo. The Goldreich's home already served as the fire brigade headquarters during the day and had a Germany army car repair shop in the yard. Now it also became a place of entertainment for the occupiers at night. According to the order, one room in the house was turned into a "pleasure" room. Every night the police commander entertained a young Polish girl who was delivered into his hands. Elza was forced to offer her bed to the debauched policeman and his girl. She had to clean the room after their wild nights and prepare meals for them when she didn't have enough food for her children.

The Jewish community building was the preferred place of entertainment for the new authorities in Turka. "This is where they ate sardines, got drunk on Hungarian liquor, and smoked tobacco. After a party, completely stuffed and drunk, they would roam the streets and torture Jews," Yona remembers.

Then the Death Truck arrived in town.

Every few days, a Gestapo truck drove through the streets. The truck stopped from time to time in front of a Jewish house, and members of the Gestapo would brutally drag out a father or mother, a son or a brother. The homeless, who had been expelled from their villages, tried to disappear into the narrow streets. They were hunted down like animals and loaded onto the truck.

The Gestapo made no distinction between men and women, children and old people, the sick or handicapped. Yona knew that every time he left the house, his life was in danger. Many Jewish women colored their hair blond, and many hurried to marry gentiles, converting to Christianity in order to save their lives.

After the truck was full, it drove out of town, its tires screeching. The Jews swallowed by the thick khaki awning that covered the Death Truck disappeared. With every round, the streets of Turka became emptier and families lost their loved ones.

The fate of those carried away by the Gestapo's Death Truck became clear when Sarah Nistel, the former butcher's wife, returned to town. "Sarah was one of twenty-five Jews abducted one day by the Gestapo and loaded onto the Death Truck," remembers Yona. "They were driven to an open field nearby, put in front of a large pit that had been dug previously and immediately shot dead. Sarah threw herself into the pit before a Nazi bullet could hit her. She remained among the dead bodies even after the Germans laid boards across the hole to cover it. Luckily for her, they did not fill it with dirt like an ordinary grave. Late at night, the butcher's wife returned to town, terrified, looking for shelter in friends' homes and telling the horrible story. To our ears, it sounded almost impossible to believe. Afterwards, the Jews in town called her 'the walking dead.'"

Sarah's story was further confirmed a few days later when a fifteen-year-old boy, Haim Shine, also came back from a massacre. "Haim was caught on the Death Truck at twilight," recounts Yona. "During the first round of shooting, a bullet grazed his ear and, full of terror, he fell into the death pit. For long hours, he suffered the pain of his wound but didn't make a sound until the Germans disappeared from the field. Only then did he crawl out from under the bodies and fled back into town to tell about the massacre. The boy led a few people to the gravesite, and there it was, the huge pit – the proof of cold-blooded murder. After a few rounds of bloodshed, the pit was filled and a sign posted there read: 'Communists are buried here.' Why would four hundred men, women and children be executed like that?"

The Nazis called the kidnapping and disappearance of Jews "actions" ("operation" in German). The expression became associated with the murder of Jews by the Nazis, with the cooperation of enthusiastic local collaborators.

Yona knew many of the victims: eighty-year-old Rabbi Meivnovitz; Jacob Rand, his Cheder's teacher; Joshua Lengenauer, his classmate; acquaintances and friends of the family. The terrible story of the pharmacist's daughter, Erika Menash, is also etched into his memory. The little girl would not let go of her mother when the Gestapo tried to kill her. In front of her father's eyes, bullets separated the daughter from her mother. Both were shot dead. The pharmacist lost his mind.

At the same time, the expulsions began. About two thousand Jews in Turka and the surrounding villages were forced to leave their homes. The homes were seized immediately by the Ukrainians. The fate of those who were expelled remained a frightful mystery that tormented the remaining Jews continuously.

Many of those who escaped the blow of expulsion fled to the forests and mountains surrounding Turka. Yet their chances of surviving the Carpathian winter in trenches they dug, or in flimsy hideouts they built among the trees, were not better than the chances of those who remained at the mercy of the Nazis in Turka.

"We were under tremendous pressure and tension. We saw that many Jews were disappearing but we didn't yet understand where they had gone," says Yona. "In June 1942, the Gestapo carried out a 'punishment action.' This time, Jews were loaded onto the Death Truck according to a list that had been prepared in advance. On that day, they murdered a hundred Jews from Turka and another sixty-five from the surrounding villages. As soon as someone's name was on the list, it did not matter what was their position, their income, or physical status. Their fate was sealed: Death. Among the victims were one of the Judenrat members, Bert Larboim; a Jewish policeman named Goldberg; Friedlich the lawyer; Yossel Birnboim the barber; and the Eiger family, with whom we were friends. The head of the Judenrat himself, Meiner, was also arrested, but saved his life at the last moment.

"We learned the reason for this punishment only a few days later. Jewish forced laborers had taken pity on the residents of the village next to their labor camp who were starving, and gave them some of their meals. For this 'offense,' a hundred and sixty-five innocent Jews were murdered."

The "actions" increased even more when summer arrived.

"Our lives became forfeit," Yona recalls. "Not a day went by, practically, without some news about someone we knew, about a family member, a relative who was expelled, forced into the ghetto or murdered. The Ukrainians, who were strongly anti-Semitic, did all the dirty work for the Germans. Without their enthusiastic assistance, the Nazi plot could not have been executed."

The Jews did not leave their homes. Danger lurked in any place, at any hour. The uncertainty caused great anxiety in the Goldreich home. The family searched for a place to hide, as primitive as it might be, from the "actions" that were still to come.

"I would ask my father, 'What will happen, Dad, what will happen?' And he would calm me down, 'Don't fear, son, we'll do something.' He tried to make us optimistic. I was a child. I listened to my parents. My father said, 'Soon the war will be over and everything will be better.' So I believed him."

Men faced the greatest danger of all. One day, all sixty-year-old men were ordered to present themselves to be "listed" in the cellar of the German police, located in a large storage room that previously had been used for building materials. Sender felt the rope was being pulled tight around his neck. He found himself a hiding place in a stable outside the house. On that day, Elza, Yona and Bumek didn't leave their tiny room and prayed that the Gestapo would pass their house by because the building served the authorities.

Every sound outside made Yona's heart race. Every door that squeaked made him jump with fear. Every window slammed shut was a sign of danger. Elza and her two sons knew that every knock on the door could bring about a tragedy. "I was afraid. We were all afraid. We understood that the situation was grave," says Yona.

One morning, Yona left their room to use the bathroom. He was in the corridor when he heard the sound of the Gestapo boots in the yard. Yona was terrified. He ran back to their room and whispered to his mother, "They are coming! They are coming!"

The soldiers noisily climbed the stairs to the second floor. Elza was gripped by fear but quickly jumped out through the window into the backyard. Yona and Bumek remained in the room, trembling with fear. They tried to disappear into a dark corner. Suddenly, the door opened with a bang. The brothers shrank back, holding onto each other tightly. A Gestapo officer fixed his eyes on the boys.

"Where are your parents?" the Gestapo officer roared in a metallic voice.

"Mom and Dad went to the Judenrat," Yona mumbled.

The Gestapo officer hesitated for a long moment and then left, slamming the door behind him.

For a few minutes, the sound of his boots could still be heard around the house. Doors were opened one after the other, and angrily slammed shut. When the Nazis left, Yona hurried to the window and peered down at the street. From the neighboring Jewish houses, entire families were taken outside. Fathers and sons, mothers and daughters were gathered in the street and led to the police station. Ukrainian militiamen shouted at them loudly, brutally hurrying them along and beating them mercilessly. The men begging and the cries of the women and children tore at Yona's heart.

Several trucks waited near the police station. The victims were loaded onto them, squeezed in like cattle fated for slaughter. After a short time, the trucks drove off. A few hours later, the trucks returned, empty. They were ready to fill again with fresh human cargo.

The "Great Action" aimed to "cleanse" Turka of most of its Jews. In the days to follow, news trickled back about the fate of the victims. The trucks stopped near the brick factory at the outskirts of town. The passengers were discharged, immediately executed in cold blood and dumped into large pits. The mass graves were filled up by more and more human corpses with every round the trucks made.

One of the saddest stories about the Great Action concerned two young brothers. Their parents were taken on the Death Truck. Desperate and crying, the boys ran after the truck. Afraid to be left behind, the brothers begged to join their parents. The truck stopped, and the policeman in charge told the boys to get onto the truck. Shortly after, as the children hugged their parents, the family was murdered together and thrown into the pit of the dead.

The Great Action continued for a number of days and achieved its goal. Turka was emptied of most of its Jews. After the mass murder, the Judenrat was ordered to collect money and possessions from the few remaining Jews to pay for the ammunition that had been used to shoot the helpless victims.

༄

After the Great Action, the murder of Jews became a daily event. Children who ventured out into the street disappeared without a trace. Mothers who left their hiding places to find food for their starving families were shot in broad daylight. Men were caught during sudden raids carried out by the German gendarmes and the Ukrainian police. No one knew if they would survive the day.

One of the Goldreichs' last friends still alive was a Jewish tinsmith. He secretly came and sealed their little hiding place on the upper floor and hid its entrance. The door was sealed and camouflaged as a wall. The tinsmith made an opening in the roof for entry and exit.

This renovation would have been impossible without the cooperation of one of the fireman, a merciful Christian, who worked on the building's first floor. The fireman looked the other way. He even gave a helping hand to his "hosts," by supplying them with a bottle of milk from his farm every morning.

As primitive and easy to find as it was, the hiding place provided a shelter that others could only dream about in the atmosphere of uncertainty and death prevailing in Turka.

In this impossible struggle for survival, Jews informed on their fellow Jews in order to postpone the inevitable for a few days. People lost faith in each other, and everyone tried to save their own life at any price.

The Goldreich's eldest son, Eizo, became the family's main source of food. Eizo defected from the Jewish Police and found shelter in the mountains. From time to time, he snuck into the town at night and went to his family's house.

He brought whatever small amount of food he managed to secure. Well before dawn, Eizo snuck back out into the street, putting himself in great danger, as he returned to his hideout.

Circumstances in the small, dark room were difficult. There was little to eat and conditions were unbearable, yet Sender and Elza still did whatever they could to help others. The room became even more crowded when two sisters, whose husbands were forced to join the Russian army, were secretly taken into the hideout.

"If we just hold on," Sender repeatedly encouraged his family and guests, "Everything will be alright. We'll return to the way it was and we will be saved."

But the news did nothing to encourage faith. The Germany army controlled most of Europe and had reached the outskirts of Moscow. The only hope was that the Allies – the United States and Great Britain – would go to war against the Nazis and prevent Hitler from taking over the entire world. The names of Winston Churchill, the British Prime Minister, and Franklin Roosevelt, the American President, became synonyms for salvation. But neither Great Britain nor the United States were in a hurry to join the battle. And even if they did go to war against the Nazis, would the Allies be able to defeat the empire of evil? Would the Jews be able to hold until then?

"President Roosevelt could have killed Hitler as soon as he took office but he didn't care about the Jews' fate," Yona recalls with frustration. "The United States even participated in the 1936 Nazi Olympic Games. Roosevelt's consultant, Joseph Kennedy,[*] who was the US Ambassador in Britain, whispered to the President, 'The Jewish problem is not our problem.' When the US Chief of Staff, George Marshall, was asked to bomb the death trains on their way to Auschwitz, in order to

---

[*] Father of President John F. Kennedy and Senators Robert and Edward Kennedy.

stop the murders – even at the price of Jews' lives – Marshall said that the bombs were needed for more important targets."

The only chance of survival was to escape across the border into Hungary. Turka's Jews fed on rumors that nothing bad was happening to Hungarian Jews. In Turka, the remaining Jews packed their few belongings and headed out, alone or in small groups, to escape across the border into Hungary, "the land of dreams." Only a few succeeded. Many were caught on the way, either on the Polish side of the border or on the Hungarian side. Many were caught by the Ukrainian militia or by cruel bands of villagers. Some were killed immediately. Others where sent to labor camps where they were murdered, died of starvation or worked to death.

Yona's uncle, Joseph Goldreich, and a small group of Jews tried to sneak from Botelka into Hungary. There is little difference between the Hungarian and the Polish landscape and they got lost on the way. A dispute ensued. Were they still in Poland? Or had they already crossed over into Hungary? Uncle Joseph spoke Hungarian and believed they were already on the Hungarian side. He volunteered to walk to a nearby village and verify their location. Uncle Joseph disappeared without a trace. Most likely, he was murdered for his worn-out suitcase and clothes.

In another case, Yona's Uncle Issachar was arrested and about to be sent to a Nazi labor camp. The surviving members of the Goldreich family assembled and pooled their few possessions in an attempt to bribe the German gendarmes to release Issachar. The meager bribe was accepted but Uncle Issachar wasn't saved. He was murdered.

The possibility of escape became the main subject of whispered conversation in the Goldreich home. The family talked, planned and dreamed in the secrecy of their sealed shelter beneath the roof. "How can it be done?" Sender wondered.

"How can a family of five go across the border? Who will take care of us later?"

"We need to find a smuggler," the others whispered to him.

Sender was concerned about putting his family into the hands of a smuggler. Stories abounded in Turka about smugglers who betrayed the trust of the Jews and turned their charges over to the Germans. Other stories told of smugglers who had even murdered the Jews under their protection.

In the beginning of the summer of 1942, Sender and Elza realized there was no time left for deliberations. A year after the Nazi occupation started, a new "action" began. It was more cruel and horrifying than anything that had taken place before. For days, the Gestapo, accompanied by their Ukrainian allies, went from house to house in an attempt to finally put an end to the Jewish presence in Turka.

Scared to death, the Goldreichs hid in their sealed, dark hideout. From the outside, they heard shots and yelling in German as the Gestapo stormed their neighbor's home. They heard the terrible cries of the Keller family as they were beaten.

When the Gestapo entered their house, the family held their breath and froze on the spot. The sound of the Gestapo's boots and their loud voices could be heard from the basement. Then the Gestapo were on the roof, right above the heads of the family hiding below. Yona believes it was a "miracle" they were not caught that day. He has no other explanation.

Later, they learned that the Jews caught in the action were lead in a small procession to the place where the great synagogue had once stood. It was now a storeroom where the Nazis kept Jewish assets. There, the Jews were "cleaned" of wedding rings, gold teeth and of any valuables they carried. From there, the Jews walked in guarded lines towards the railway. They were crowded onto cattle wagons and sent on their way to the unknown. Rumors had it that they were buried alive in mass graves.

Several days later, the Goldreichs came out of their hiding place. The firemen on the first floor were stunned to see that the owners of the house, who had hidden above their heads, were still alive.

The Goldreichs were one of the few Jewish families remaining in Turka. Yona's Uncle Joshua Erdman, a member of the Judenrat, was also still alive. Uncle Erdman visited their room but he did not have good news. "By winter, no Jews will be left around Turka," said Uncle Erdman with a long face. "The Germans already wiped out ninety percent of us. Those who won't flee will die."

Uncle Erdman, unfortunately, knew what he was talking about. A short time later, he was expelled from his office and shared the fate of most Jews in Turka: death.

Sender hurried to finish planning his family's escape to Hungary. A number of relatives lived there and he hoped to receive help from them. Time was running out. Another winter was approaching. If they didn't escape now, they might never be able to do so.

CHAPTER FOUR

The deal to smuggle the Goldreich family to Hungary was cut in whispers, behind closed doors. Although Hungary was an ally of Nazi Germany, the situation of the Hungarian Jews was far better during the first years of the war than that of Jews in the territories under German occupation. The Hungarian Jews' rights were revoked, but at least their lives were not in danger. "Miklós Horthy, the Fascist President of Hungary, made a deal with the Nazi regime according to which they wouldn't harm the Jews in Hungary," Yona explains.

The illusion of stability and security that prevailed among the Hungarian Jews led Sender to believe his family would find shelter there from the Nazi terror. Yet, getting to Hungary was not an easy operation. Crossing the border was extremely dangerous. On the Polish side of the border, the Nazis hunted down Jews who tried to escape. "The Ukrainian gentiles also persecuted the Jews, abused them, robbed them and handed them over to the Nazis," Yona elaborates. On the Hungarian side, the Fascist militias did not hesitate to shoot the miserable refugees.

Approximately sixty Jews from Turka tried to get across the border to Hungary. Many were shot on the way by Nazi or

Hungarian soldiers. Others were lynched after being discovered by villagers along the border. Some were killed by the smugglers themselves.

Sender had a cousin in Mukachevo, a small town in western Hungary (today in Ukrainian territory), about 75 miles (120 kilometers) from Turka. This cousin, Michael Goldreich, and his wife were the owners of a bicycle shop in the town's market. Sender made his final decision. They had to run from Poland as fast as possible and reach Mukachevo.

For days, he looked for a reliable and courageous smuggler to take them across the border. Someone he could trust. Eventually he found his man: a Communist who considered the Nazis enemies and the smuggling of people across the border a kind of battle against them. The man had already successfully accompanied a number of Jewish families from Turka to the other side. Sender decided to put his faith in him. The smuggler, however, had second thoughts about taking the entire family of five together. Therefore, two operations were agreed upon: First, the children would escape, and then, when the smuggler returned safely, he would accompany Sender and Elza.

Sender ordered his children to keep the plan a complete secret. Yona was warned not to utter a word about the impending flight. In starving Turka, only a few hundred Jews remained and there was hardly a family that was still intact. Anyone, even a close friend, was liable to snitch in return for a slice of bread.

"The children will go first, and you will look after them," Sender instructed his eldest son, Eizo, who was nearly seventeen.

But Eizo refused to join his brothers. "I won't leave you here alone," he told his parents. "What if Mother needs help on the long trip? I will escape with you on the second run."

"Yona and Bumek are too young," Elza tried to object. "How will they set out on the dangerous journey on their own?"

Time was pressing. Winter was right around the corner. If they did not reach a decision fast, they would be stuck in Turka. Sender and Elza knew if the family stayed in town, they would go to a certain death. Still, they hesitated for a long time. How could they let their young sons face this danger alone? And yet they had no real choice. It was one of the hardest decisions any parent can make. In the end, Sender chose the painful solution to send Yona and Bumek on their way by themselves. The brothers were leaving home without their father's protection and their mother's loving, watchful eyes. Their parents were about to send them to break the law and cross the border, without passports and without permits. Sender and Elza were only too aware of the fate awaiting Polish refugees caught stealing across the border. Sender was afraid he would never see his two sons again, but he kept it to himself.

Sender decided to share the secret with their friends, the Kornhoisers, who lived in a neighboring village. Sender offered to pay for the escape of their son, Jacob, who was a few years older than Yona. In return, Jacob would look after the two Goldreich boys until they reached Mukachevo.

The countdown began and so did Elza's tears. She prepared knapsacks for Yona and Bumek. They still had a few pieces of hidden jewelry. Elza took out some gold jewelry and rings studded with diamonds, and secured them in hidden pockets she had sewn into the boys' travel clothes. She collected food to sustain them on their way. Elza was gripped by the fear of the danger and uncertainty.

At first, Elza cried in secret. As the time of the boys' departure came closer, their mother's crying became uncontrollable and heart-breaking. "In the last days before we left, she demanded that Bumek and I sleep next to her," Yona recalls.

Sender, too, had a hard time concealing the pain of a father about to let his young children go off without his protection on a dangerous journey.

In preparation for the trip, Sender insisted that Yona and Bumek change their appearance to look like gentiles, so they would not arouse suspicion. Yona and Bumek were used to wearing good jackets and hand-made wool sweaters. From now on, they were to dress in sloppy and roughly-made clothes which gave them the unkempt look of gentile peasants.

The night before their departure was emotional. Sender took out the large family album. Yona remembers, "A family album was very precious. In those days, it was a big deal to have one's photo taken, and every photograph demanded meticulous planning. Not everyone could afford this luxury. Our album contained photos of the entire family; pictures of my mom and dad, my brothers, my grandparents, uncles and cousins."

Sender showed Yona and Bumek where he would hide the family's photo album. They climbed up to the attic and Sender hid the album in a concealed niche. "In a month or two, when the war is over, we'll return home and remember that the album is hidden here," Sender told his sons.

Yona will never forget the day of his departure. In the morning, his mother made sure he was dressed properly. Even in the summer, the nights were cold in Ukraine. In particular, she made sure that he put on the thick woolen socks she had knitted. She guided his hands across the hidden pockets she had sewn into his clothes and his coat. He could feel the gold chains and the rings concealed in their folds. She showed Yona all she had put into the knapsacks: bread, cheese and some other groceries, a few pieces of clothing, his report card from school, and a number of family photos. It was the absolute minimum so that the load would not be too heavy on his shoulders.

At midday, the hour arrived. Yona remembers his mother's tight hug, her fluttering heart, and her tears that stuck to his face. It was hard for Elza to let him go, as if she were afraid this was the last time she would hug him. Yona didn't understand why parting was such a difficult affair and why his mother would not release her embrace. After all, their father promised that within two weeks they would be reunited in Hungary, the "land of freedom." His father said it would be no more than a month, perhaps two months at most before they would be together again.

"We have to go now," Sender rushed his children. Yona took one last look at the house he had been born in then hurried after his father. Sender, Eizo, Yona and Bumek snuck along backyards and narrow streets until they reached the grove outside town where they swiftly disappeared among the trees.

The meeting with the smuggler had been set for the village where the Kornhoisers lived. The walk through the fields and bypaths at the edge of the grove took a few hours. When the "delegation" from Turka reached the Kornhoiser's home, their friends were tensely waiting in the backyard of their house. The sun was already setting.

It was time to say goodbye. Unlike his mother who had almost collapsed with sorrow and anguish, Sender was decisive and practical. For the first time, he informed Yona about the possibility that their reunion in Hungary might not happen within a short period of time.

"If, for any reason, we aren't able to join you," Sender said to his son, "the most important thing is to show confidence. Don't let anybody pity you. Use the gold and the diamond rings to buy food and find a place to hide. Whatever happens, whatever will be, always remember you can't stay a child forever. You can't live without working, and you should study hard. The only treasure that can never be taken from you is what you have in your head."

Night fell and the smuggler showed up. Sender spent a few minutes with him to work out the terms and conditions of payment, and to make sure the smuggler would return to Turka to pick up the rest of the family. The smuggler was impatient. He worried about wasting the night and wanted to leave immediately.

Yona's last goodbye to his father was short. Sender again whispered to him, "Remember, my son, don't let anybody pity you."

Sender and Eizo turned back towards Turka. They hoped to reach it before sunrise and the Nazis' morning patrols. Violating the nightly curfew was an offense punishable by immediate execution. At the same time, Yona, Bumek and Jacob Kornhoiser hurried in the opposite direction, trying to catch up with the smuggler.

The little band of fugitives passed quickly by the ski resort Shimonka. It had not been active since the war began. The skies were dark and there were no stars between the clouds to light the way. The smuggler instructed them to walk in a single line. He led the way, followed by Bumek, Yona and Kornhoiser, each in the footsteps of the one in front of him. They walked quickly towards the forest on top of the hill.

All night long, they marched surreptitiously along the paths leading through the forest. Without rest, Yona concentrated on his steps and made sure to stay close to his little brother who walked in front of him. Yona's leg muscles hurt from the effort of marching relentlessly. Yet he did not make a sound. When the first light came up, the smuggler stopped. He told them to get off the path and hide inside a thicket.

"You'll hide here all day," he ordered them. "I am leaving and will be back at nightfall." He quickly disappeared among the trees.

The day seemed like an eternity as they waited for the smuggler's return. Would he be back at all? Could he be trusted? Maybe he changed his mind. Maybe he preferred to hand them over to the bloodthirsty Germans. Maybe he'd betray them to anti-Semitic villagers who would soon emerge from the trees, accompanied by their dogs with sharp teeth. Yona could not fall asleep. Every whisper of the wind frightened him. He jumped with horror at every moving shadow caused by the sun's rays. All day he carefully kept watch over his little brother who hid beside him in the bush. From now on, he was responsible for Bumek. He not only had to save himself, but also his little brother.

Night fell and the smuggler didn't appear. Why didn't he come? Maybe something had happened to him. Maybe he had been captured himself. If he did not come back, Yona had no idea where they were and which way to return home. Soon it would be impossible to see even a meter away in the dark.

The smuggler appeared as suddenly as he had disappeared. Without missing a beat, he ordered the boys to follow him. The journey continued.

In the course of the second night, the smuggler increased his speed. The children were almost forced to run in order to keep up. On the right, not too far from them, they could see the glittering lights of a small village. The smuggler's rapid pace was intended to pass it as quickly as possible, lest dogs there pick up the infiltrators' scent and expose them by barking. Yona knew only too well what would happen if the villagers detected them. As they moved past, they heard a few barks behind them. The group moved even faster.

At first daylight, they again moved into a thicket. The boys fell down exhausted among the high trees. This time, the smuggler stayed with them and he quickly fell into a slumber. In spite of his exhaustion, Yona was unable to sleep on the second day either.

Night after night they marched onward, hiding during the day. On the sixth day the smuggler informed them, "Tonight, we cross the border."

This was the most difficult and dangerous part of their march. Before they set out, the smuggler demanded that Yona and Bumek show him the contents of their knapsacks. Without saying a word, he pulled out the school report cards and the family photos. "I'll hide these here and return them to your parents," he said. Yona's heart broke at the sudden loss of these tangible connections to his past and his family.

Before they started walking, the smuggler warned them, "The Germans and the Ukrainians are patrolling the entire area. After we cross the border, there will be Hungarian soldiers. Any of them will be happy to kill us if they get the opportunity. Remember, once we are in Hungary, you must not speak a word of Polish!"

The refugees advanced along a narrow trail. The march on this last night was more difficult than it had been during the preceding nights. The trail curved along an ascending slope. The heavy breathing caused by the children's climbing efforts could be heard from afar.

They had crossed the border into Hungary when the smuggler suddenly stopped short. His urgent whispers rushed them to hide among the trees at the side of the path. Frightened, they swiftly hopped into a thicket. Yona curled up behind the trunk of a thick tree, covering his brother. They froze in position and held their breath.

From behind a bend in the path, a squad of Hungarian guards appeared. Their eyes tried to break through the darkness and their rifles were at the ready.

The guards stopped directly in front of the refugees' hiding place. Yona's heart skipped a beat. It seemed that one of the guards was looking straight at him. The soldiers exchanged words between themselves in a language unknown to the boys.

Had they been discovered? Had they been caught? Had their hour of death arrived?

For a few minutes, which felt like an eternity, the soldiers scanned the area. Finally, they moved on. Time went slowly as the sound of the Hungarian soldiers' steps faded into the distance and finally disappeared. The smuggler silently signaled for the boys to follow him.

At the end of that long and tense night, the group once again found a hiding place. As daylight came, the young infiltrators hungrily searched for scraps of leftover food in their knapsacks. They waited for night to fall.

Although Yona was well aware their lives were still in danger, he felt relieved, almost at ease. They had crossed the border into Hungary – the "land of safety."

As night fell, the euphoria evaporated. New dangers faced them. After the long march, the little group was to continue by train towards the final destination of their escape – the town of Mukachevo.[*]

The train station's platform was crowded with new recruits of the Hungarian army. The smuggler was overcome with fear that someone might identify the boys as Jews. He ordered Yona, Bumek and Kornhoiser to split up and move away from each other. When the train arrived, they were to board on their own and stay apart. The smuggler told them to get lost among the mob and remain hidden from the conductor's eyes.

They boarded the train separately. The trip took all night on the train loaded with Hungarian soldiers, many of whom were drunk. Yona disappeared into a crowded railcar and

---

[*] At the time, there were about forty thousand residents in Mukachevo; half of them were Jews.

avoided curious eyes. All through the long journey, Yona tried to remain invisible. He worried about his brother's safety.

As soon as the train stopped at the railway station in Mukachevo, Yona rushed to find Bumek. Together, the brothers pushed through the drunken soldiers' sweaty bodies and stepped off the train onto the station's platform. With a sigh of relief, they spotted the smuggler and Kornhoiser.

The smuggler rushed his "cargo" to the address he had been given: Michael Goldreich's bicycle shop. As they walked through Mukachevo, Yona looked around in wonder. It was the first time in his life that he had seen a town so large and modern. As they walked through the streets, Yona was also amazed to encounter Jews who were not afraid to show their religion. He was surprised to see the long beards, side locks and tzitziot, the fringes of their ritual undergarment, peeking out of their clothes. Ever since the Nazi occupation, no Jew in Turka dared to walk around like that.

After six nights of marching seventy-five miles through forests, and six days of broken sleep, the band of fugitives arrived at the market in Mukachevo. The smuggler quickly spotted Michael Goldreich's bicycle shop. Yona and Bumek finally reached their destination.

Michael Goldreich and his wife received them with open arms. The couple hastily led the worn-out refugees to the shop's small storeroom. Michael quietly exchanged whispers with the smuggler. Michael tore apart a large banknote and put one half in an envelope. Yona added a handwritten note in Yiddish. This was to serve as proof for his parents that the boys had arrived safely. If the smuggler returned with the rest of the family, he would get the second half of the banknote. The smuggler concealed the envelope in his clothes and hastily left.

The three survivors crowded into the back storeroom of the bicycle shop. The boys were exhausted, but were safe and sound. After all the tension, anxiety and sleepless days, they fell into a deep slumber.

The day after their arrival, Jacob Kornhoiser parted from Yona and Bumek. Kornhoiser had fulfilled his obligation to watch over the boys until they reached their uncle's home.[*]

The joy of arriving in Mukachevo was short-lived. The harsh reality for illegal immigrants was a life of fear. Illegal immigrants had to constantly change hiding places and were always on the run from informers and anyone wearing a uniform.

Yona and Bumek didn't know a word in Hungarian. They were warned not to move around alone outside and to keep away from strangers. Mainly, they were to keep their mouths shut and not speak Polish in public. "If an officer stops you in the street and asks you something in Hungarian, you will not understand what he says. He'll immediately know that you are not from around here, and you'll be expelled back to Poland," said Michael's wife.

"This verdict was pretty hard on us," Yona recalls. "Hungarian is a difficult language, which does not have anything in common with any other language. It was impossible to improvise or fake an accent in Hungarian."

When Yona told his cousin's family and the Jews at the synagogue about events in Turka they refused to believe him. They couldn't accept Yona's account of the executions, mass graves and the cruel extermination of most of the Jews. "The boy is probably making it up. He's exaggerating," they said behind his back. "He suffers from a vivid imagination."

But Yona knew that danger lurked everywhere, even in Mukachevo. It came from greedy Jews and collaborators, from jealous neighbors and from anti-Semitic gentiles.

---

[*] Kornhoiser eventually managed to reach the United States. He has never forgotten the Goldreichs who funded his escape and saved his life.

The Hungarian police were only too aware of the waves of refugees pouring in from Poland. The police carried out sudden raids on homes and combed the streets for infiltrators and illegal aliens. The fact that they did not speak Hungarian made the boys an especially easy target.

Michael and his wife were afraid to keep Yona and Bumek in their home which was located in the center of town. They made arrangements for the brothers to find shelter at the synagogue during the day, in the custody of the elderly Rabbi Baruch Yehoshua Yerachmimel Rabinovitch. At night, the boys were taken to the home of a Jewish widow on the outskirts of town. They slept in a pit that had been dug next to the house.

All Yona and Bumek could do now was wait for their parents and Eizo. Every morning, they awoke with intense expectations. They hoped this would be the day or the night their father, mother and brother would arrive and the family would be reunited. Yona sent a postcard every day to his parents, "We arrived safely. We are waiting for you in Mukachevo." But days went by, then one week and another. The loneliness, pressure and tension were a heavy load. Their family didn't arrive and the boys didn't receive any sign of life from them.

A terrible fear started to fill Yona's heart. Was it possible that his parents had not succeeded in crossing the border? Endless scenarios rushed through his mind. Maybe the smuggler was caught on his way back… Maybe their parents and brother were suspected after Yona and Bumek disappeared… Maybe they were arrested along the way… Yona didn't dare think about the worst scenario but he began to realize it was possible that he and Bumek were alone in the world. Yona was the older brother and he would have to take responsibility for their safety.

Yona knew their presence in Mukachevo was not only dangerous for him and Bumek, but also for their hosts. If the brothers stayed in Mukachevo, they would be captured sooner or later. Everyone who had helped hide them would be at risk. Michael's wife couldn't hide her fear, "They will kill us all." Yona worried about Michael, his cousin's wife, the Rabbi, the people at the synagogue, the widow at whose premises Yona and Bumek spent the night, and other good Jews who hosted them from time to time. If any of these people were caught helping the brothers, their fate would be brutal: death. The bleak situation forced Yona to look for an alternative plan.

Yona remembered his father's farewell words, "The most important thing is to show confidence. Do not let anyone pity you." So, almost a month after the boys crossed the border into Hungary, Yona settled on a new plan of action. Mukachevo was larger than Turka but it was not big enough for the boys to disappear in the crowd. Yona knew nothing about Budapest but he felt their chances of survival would be much higher in a bigger city.

"We are going to Budapest. When our parents arrive, please tell them that we are waiting there," Yona told his cousin.

Michael listened seriously to the determined boy. Yona did not talk as a child speaks to an adult, but as a man to a man. Yona put a gold chain from the hidden pockets into Michael's hand. "Buy us tickets to Budapest," Yona pleaded.

In the following days, Michael exchanged the gold chain for Hungarian money and bought tickets for them on a train going directly to Budapest. Michael also recruited a young Jew to accompany the brothers on their way. The night before departure, their young companion took the brothers to his house. Once again, Yona spent a sleepless night. His thoughts raced, "What would they find in Budapest? What happened to their parents and Eizo? What did life hold in store for him?"

The express train from Mukachevo to Budapest left on time. Yona and Bumek were already familiar with the required behavior: They did not say a word, remained inconspicuous and tried their best not to arouse suspicion. The train went past forests, rivers, towns and villages.

The two boys were thrilled when they left the train station in Budapest. The big city spread across both banks of the Danube River. As their young escort led them along the busy streets, Yona was amazed at the historic monuments. There were basilicas, fortresses, palaces, sculptures, impressive apartment buildings, plazas, squares, fountains, and shop windows displaying objects and clothes unlike those seen in Turka. Yona noticed that most shops had Jewish names. The streetcars carrying passengers along the crowded streets were a wonder of technology. For the first time in his life, Yona experienced the atmosphere of a large metropolis and felt the energy of more than one million people hurrying around.

Their escort led them quickly towards the Great Synagogue located on Dohany Street in the center of the city's Jewish community.[*] The Synagogue is famous for its architecture, which combines Gothic, Moorish and Byzantine elements. Yona and Bumek looked in astonishment at the amazing facade and the two towers rising high above the house of prayer. Before they could catch their breath, their escort departed. The two brothers were left on their own. Yona and Bumek were not the first refugees to find shelter at the synagogue. The place was packed with Jews who had fled from all over Eastern Europe. But the helpless management of the synagogue didn't quite know what to do with the two Polish children left in their care and, like most Hungarian Jews, they did not speak Yiddish. Luckily, Yona's mother had taught him German and Yona was able to communicate with the synagogue officials.

---

[*] Budapest's Jews had created a unique conservative in Judaism, called Neology. The visionary of the Jewish State, Theodor Herzl, identified himself with this stream, and was educated at the Great Synagogue school in the early twentieth century. Neology came to its end several years later.

Yona repeatedly told about the massacre in Turka and the story of the boys' escape. In Budapest, as in Mukachevo, he faced doubtful glances. "The boy is making things up. He doesn't know what he is saying," was the common reaction. The apathy of the Hungarian Jews deeply upset Yona. "We were only a few hours away from the Polish border and from Turka, and people had no idea of what was happening across the border. The Hungarian Jews were complacent. They didn't believe that genocide was underway over the borders of the country. And they didn't realize that sooner or later the war would reach them as well. Two years later, it happened, and Adolf Eichmann started implementing the Final Solution in their country, too."

On his first day in Budapest, Yona befriended a refugee from the region of Turka. Their new friend led the brothers to the home of a good-hearted widow who hid Jewish refugees in one room of her house where she had squeezed nine beds. About an hour before sunrise, the widow woke them up and hurried them to leave so that the neighbors would not get suspicious. The two children then went back to the synagogue where they found shelter during the day.

Although they didn't speak Hungarian, the lure of going outside overcame the fear that they might be arrested, revealed as refugees, expelled to Poland and handed over to the Nazis. With the innocence of small-town boys, Yona and Bumek roamed the streets of the big city. They were so fascinated by the sights they forgot about the danger that threatened them. "When Bumek saw the street car, he climbed on it excitedly, as a child who stumbles upon a new toy," Yona recalls. "He did not comprehend how dangerous it would be if the conductor stopped him."

In the following days, the two gradually picked up some basic words in Hungarian and copied the behavior of the Hungarian children.

The synagogue provided them with food and a little money but their assets started to run out. And as yet another week went by without any sign of life from their parents or brother, the boys' worries about their family's fate became unbearable. Yona immediately questioned every new refugee arriving at the synagogue about where he had come from and what he knew.

The synagogue in Budapest was bursting at the seams from the flow of arriving refugees. And the synagogue officials still didn't know what to do with two Polish boys waiting for parents who might never show up. Yona discovered that a cousin had found shelter in Neertehest, another town in Hungary. Yona asked the synagogue council to assist him with funding for a trip to Neertehest. The council complimented him on the idea and one of the council members was appointed to accompany the children to their destination. Within a few hours, Yona and Bumek boarded the train, hoping to find their cousin.

During the trip, Yona was wide awake and alert. He and Bumek did not say a word. Their escort kept his eyes on them constantly. Through the window of the train, Yona watched the landscape pass by. He was jolted by a strong feeling of déjà vu. The landscape looked just like the countryside they had traversed on their way from Mukachevo to Budapest. Suddenly, Yona realized they were being sent back to Mukachevo. Yona suppressed his anger and didn't show how much it hurt his feelings. Instead, Yona immediately planned his next move. He quickly whispered to Bumek, telling him what was really going on. When the train stopped at the station before Mukachevo, in the little town of Chopp, Yona and Bumek clutched their stomachs. They "urgently needed" to go to the restroom.

"We will be back right away," Yona told their escort. The boys left their knapsacks in his hands for safekeeping. Yona hurried his brother along and they jumped off the train.

By the time the escort realized the two had run away, Yona and Bumek were racing toward the center of town. Behind them, the train's whistle signaled it was leaving the station.

Lost and with no possessions, Yona did not lose his head. He had already gained experience in being on the road. He looked for a synagogue. After wandering around the town, Yona discovered a small building which served as a Yeshiva. The two boys entered the building at the height of the *Minha* afternoon prayers. At first, no one in the congregation noticed them. Once the prayers were over, some of the young students noticed them and approached. Yona told again about the annihilation of the Jewish community in Turka, and about their escape from Poland. The Yeshiva students also found it hard to believe, yet agreed to help them.

Purchasing a train ticket required not only presenting an identity card, preferably a Hungarian one, but also money which the brothers didn't have. "Charity saves lives," said the Yeshiva students. The students quickly raised money and purchased the tickets back to Budapest.

Yona and Bumek left on the return train that very night. They disappeared into a large crowd of Slovakian soldiers who were insulting and cursing Jews. Yona signaled his little brother to pretend that he was sleeping. Yona closed his eyes too and ignored the hateful words around him.

They next day they arrived back at Budapest. The two lonely children were all by themselves in the bustling city and had nothing to their names.

Yona didn't even consider going back to the Jewish community that had deceptively tried to send them back to Mukachevo. He decided to look for help in an orthodox synagogue. The orthodox Jews spoke Yiddish, a language he knew, and Yona would be able to manage more easily. As they encountered more and more people in the streets wearing kaftans and shtreimels (traditional fur hats), Yona knew they were getting closer. Thus they found their new home.

Jews are compassionate and many good people helped Yona and Bumek, whether with good advice, modest aid, or an invitation to Sabbath dinner. Still, this was not sufficient to calm the boys' worries. The traumatic events they had lived through kept them from adopting the sense of security that prevailed among Hungarian Jews.

These experiences forced Yona to mature quickly. He organized a place for them to sleep, and worked at odd jobs to earn some money. He found new friends and started speaking a little Hungarian. Every day he spent time at synagogues. He found more and more good people who would host them in their homes and feed them. But mostly, he kept his eyes and ears open.

As more news came about the mass murders of Poland's Jews by the Nazis, his fears increased. Each day, he spent hours talking to refugees who gathered in the synagogues, trying to get any information about his family.

A refugee who came from Mukachevo told Yona that he had seen his parents there. One night, Yona was informed by the synagogue manager that his parents had telephoned from the post office in Mukachevo and "they were on their way." That night Yona and Bumek were so excited they didn't get a moment of sleep. But days went by and no one came.

Then Yona met a refugee from the region of Turka who told him that no Jews were left in their home town. Shortly after Yona and Bumek escaped, the Gestapo executed the Final Action. Hearing this testimony, Yona realized his parents and brother were not seen again in Turka. His face went pale, and Bumek burst into tears.

A few days later, an exhausted refugee from Poland reported that a large group of Jews from Turka had tried to get across the border. Based on his description, it seemed likely that Sender, Elza and Eizo were among them. "Nobody knows the fate of that group," the man whispered.

Yona suddenly remembered the name of a Hungarian friend of the family who lived in Budapest. He was the father-in-law of a well known dentist. With his newfound resourcefulness, Yona tracked down the man's address and set out with Bumek to meet him. The man remembered the Goldreich family and welcomed the boys warmly. When he heard what they had been through, he was alarmed and quickly contacted an acquaintance in one of the towns along the border. The acquaintance soon got back to him with bad news.

"Your parents and Eizo succeeded in getting across the border safely. They even managed to reach Mukachevo but they were caught immediately after their arrival. Someone must have informed on them," the friend told the shocked children. "They were handed over to the German police."

The man didn't have to say any more. Bumek burst into tears. Yona held back his own tears but his heart was broken. Could it really be that they would never see their family again? And what would happen now to his little brother and himself? Then the community Rabbi handed the boys a postcard that had arrived mysteriously. It was written in German in their father's handwriting. The postcard said they had crossed the border and been caught. Yona read the worn postcard over and over again. He was afraid of the worst but still refused to give up hope. Maybe a miracle had happened. Maybe, through an act of God, his parents and Eizo had been able to escape from hell.

The boys were broken-hearted and stricken with grief. Yona and Bumek huddled in a synagogue corner, ignoring the words of condolence and encouragement from the other refugees. They had been on the road for months. They were constantly running, hiding and living from hand to mouth. What would become of them now?

The orthodox community where Yona and Bumek stayed was not Zionist, but a new wave started sweeping the synagogue in the fall of 1942. Rumors of a new possibility restored some of Yona's hope.

The Bureau of the Land of Israel (also known as "The Palestine Office") had re-opened in Budapest. It was run by a representative of the HaPoel HaMizrahi movement, Dr. Moshe (Miklosh) Krauss. The Palestine Office represented the executive branch of the Zionist Organization and its main objective was to promote Jewish settlement in Palestine.

Prior to June 1941, there had been a wave of Jewish immigration from Hungary to Palestine, motivated by Zionist ideology. After all, Budapest was the birthplace of the visionary of the Jewish State, Theodor Herzl. But when Hungary joined Nazi Germany and broke off relations with the Allies, the British Embassy in Hungary closed down, and no more permits were issued to immigrate to Palestine.

Yona heard about a deal between the British and Hungarians. According to this agreement, the British would release wounded Hungarian captives. In return, the Hungarian authorities would allow a group of fifty Jewish orphans to leave for Palestine where the Jewish community promised to accept them. The British, who ruled over Palestine, would provide immigration permits through the neutral Swiss Embassy. It was clearly a dangerous adventure which required going through German occupied territories. Would the Nazis respect the agreement?

Yona and Bumek presented themselves at the Bureau of the Land of Israel. Krauss and his men were impressed by the two Jewish boys who had survived against all odds. Yet it was not so easy to help them. Yona and Bumek did not fit the criteria for joining the trip. They were not Hungarian, which was preferable. They were both younger than the minimum required age of sixteen. Even if they could get past these obstacles, the competition for the fifty places was fierce.

Yona decided that these obstacles would not stop them. He and Bumek must be included on the list of passengers, no matter what. Yona started the battle of his life. He would use his charm, his stubbornness and his fierce determination. He would do whatever it took to get them on that train to freedom.

CHAPTER FIVE

Yona spent most of his time at the Palestine Office. He was determined to find a way for them to escape from Hungary and from the terrible war raging across Europe. A lonely, fifteen-year-old Jewish boy, possibly an orphan, created a "lobby" for himself in a strange and unknown place – without even being able to speak the local language.

Yona hid his feelings and kept a stoic face, yet he was full of fear. Almost six months had passed since the brothers escaped from Turka. It had been two months since he heard about the phone call from his parents and received the wrinkled postcard from their father. Since then, there had been no sign of life from his parents or older brother.

Yona bore a great responsibility on his shoulders, not only for himself but also for his little brother for whom he had become a father figure. Yona did not share the shocking news arriving from the front lines with Bumek. Indeed, he made an effort to hide the news about the tens of thousands of casualties, and the mass murders of Jews in their country. Family by family, village by village, ghetto by ghetto, the Jews of Poland were annihilated. Every day and every sleepless night, Yona was also consumed with doubts and uncertainty about the fate of his parents and Eizo. These fears only increased Yona's feeling that, if he did not find a way to escape from Europe, the brothers' fate would be the same as all the Jews from their home country.

For Yona, Palestine was the other side of the universe. It was light years away from the fields of war and the horrible memories he carried. The journey to Palestine, as dangerous as it might be, was their only chance to survive.

Yona identified the decision makers in the Palestine Office, and those in charge of approving the quota of teenagers going to Palestine. Then he got to work. He turned to the leaders of the Jewish community and asked them to use their influence to add his brother and himself to the list. He went to the Palestine Office every day. He lobbied each clerk individually, trying to convince them it was absolutely vital for him and his brother to be included on the list of passengers.

At the Palestine Office he stumbled upon an unexpected obstacle: The Bureau of the Land of Israel had decided to allow only one member of a family to be included in the quota. They were inclined to take the brothers' situation under consideration and let some criteria slide, but they determinedly refused to have the two brothers embark on a dangerous journey together.

Yona did not have to think at all, "My brother Bumek shall go." However, there was still a problem. The required minimum age was sixteen. Bumek was not yet thirteen and thus did not meet the immigration criteria.

"Then you go," the clerk suggested to Yona. But Yona would not consider the possibility of leaving his brother behind.

Yona fought fervently. He accosted officials. He tried explaining, begging and pleading. "Sorry," they told him. "We only take one child per family."

"How can I leave my brother here alone?" protested Yona. "He's a little boy who does not speak Hungarian. We have no parents here, no home. What would become of him?" Yona also discarded the idea of sending his brother alone. "How can I send Bumek alone to an unknown country? And what would happen to me all alone in Hungary? You must take us both!"

But, as the quota of passengers filled up, Yona realized they both might miss the train. He could not let that happen. He hated the thought of being separated from his brother but made up his mind that he would fight to at least have Bumek included on the list. Yona convinced the clerks at the Palestine Office to forge Bumek's age. The clerk looked at the scrawny kid and seemed skeptical that the "trick" would work. Yet Yona did not waver until he got the required signature that added Bumek to the list.

The moment Bumek understood that he was going to Palestine alone, he was gripped by fear. "Where is Palestine anyway?" Bumek declared he would not leave without his brother. The more they were refused, the more stubborn Bumek became, "I am not going alone!"

"For long days, we loitered on the building's stairs," remembers Yona. "We roamed around the corridors between the offices, among the clerks, for hours. Bumek cried while I pleaded, argued and explained. We were rejected again and again. Yet I did not give up. I would rest for awhile on the stairs outside, gather up strength and go back in."

In the meantime, the quota of boys and girls was close to being filled. The original intent was to send only Hungarian children to Palestine but the local Jews did not stand in line. They feared the dangerous journey and were still under the impression that no one in Hungary would harm them. So new criteria was used. The passengers were selected on the basis of the degree of danger they faced. Most of them were refugees, like Yona and Bumek, from Poland and Czechoslovakia. All who were chosen to go on the journey had one thing in common: their parents had disappeared in the war.

The date of departure had been determined and was fast approaching: the frozen December of 1942.

The clerks sympathized with Yona's request to join his brother but there was nothing they could do. "It is impossible," they kept repeating. The rule was "one per family." In any case, the demand was far greater than the numbers of permits available.

"Maybe you will join the next train," they tried to comfort Yona.

"I will not be separated from my brother, and my brother will not be separated from me!" Yona insisted fiercely.

One morning, Yona and Bumek appeared, as usual, in front of the doors of the Bureau. One of the clerks signaled for them to enter the office of the Bureau Head, Mr. Krauss.

"We are all alone in the world. All the Jews in our town were annihilated," Yona quickly started his rationale. "We have nowhere to sleep, we eat at a different place every day, we do not speak Hungarian. But we are together, for better or for worse. How can I stay behind alone? My life is in danger here in Budapest. And how will my brother be able to manage alone when just this week he should be celebrating his Bar Mitzvah?"

"Bar Mitzvah?" Krauss jumped off his chair and approached Bumek. "Let our enemies be destroyed in wrath. Mazel Tov!"

From the expression on Mr. Krauss' face, Yona suspected the boys might have won their struggle. After a long moment, Mr. Krauss reached his decision. "I have decided to send the both of you." Mr. Krauss turned to Bumek and asked affectionately, "Well, do you know your Hapatorah yet?"

The same kind Jews who had taken the boys in and helped feed them were also helping prepare Bumek for his Bar Mitzvah. Mr. Krauss, in his excitement, gave Bumek a watch as a present for his Bar Mitzvah. It was the first one Bumek ever owned.

"Moshe Krauss was a great Zionist, a dear, righteous man who saved me and my brother," recalls Yona. "Mr. Krauss did this despite the rules issued by the Jewish Agency which permitted only children sixteen and older, and only one person per family, to be evacuated. During the entire waiting period, Mr. Krauss and his men made sure we had clothes, a little money and food stamps."

Bumek's Bar Mitzvah took place on the Sabbath at the orthodox synagogue. Bumek was called to the Torah, accompanied by his brother, Yona, who stood in for their father. The ongoing sorrow they felt about their parents' and older brother's absence saddened him but Yona tried to hide his feelings from Bumek who was surrounded by the joyous crowd.

At the end of the ceremony the brothers were brought to the house of a great Rabbi, the Admor of Vizhnitz. They joined a long line of people at the door. When the boys' turn came, they were brought into a large room. The old Rabbi nodded when he heard they were on their way to Palestine. "May you succeed and have a good life," he murmured as he blessed the two brothers.

༄

Budapest, December 1942. On the eve of their departure on the long and dangerous journey, Yona and his brother were given Hungarian passports. The photographs were their own and had been taken a couple of days earlier but the names were false Hungarian names. Other details had been forged by the Zionist underground in Budapest. The brothers were required to repeat these details over and over until they knew them by heart. Any slip of the tongue or the slightest mistake when answering questions at the borders could cost them their lives, as well as the lives of the other refugees with them.

Although Budapest was not their home and had been only a temporary shelter, there were many who shed a tear the night Yona and Bumek left. The tragic story of the two brothers had touched numerous hearts, and many were impressed by Yona's maturity and wisdom. They said goodbye to the community that had welcomed them and to the young Polish refugees with whom they had become friends. They also said goodbye to the clerks at the Palestine Office who had, in the end, done more than their share to keep the two brothers together. As their departure drew closer, many Jews gave Yona notes, inscribed with their wishes, to be placed on the Western Wall* in Jerusalem. They even paid Yona with Hungarian money for that future gesture. "I thought, what would I do with Hungarian money in Israel?" Yona chuckles. "So I gave all the money to the refugee children who stayed in Hungary and could not board the train."

On the designated day, Yona collected their few possessions into one bundle. At the appointed hour, he and his brother arrived at the train station. Other youngsters were accompanied by their families or by friends. Most of them were crying, and some tried to change their minds at the last moment. Yona and Bumek, already experienced in riding trains and used to not having any relatives with them, hurried to get on the train.

The railway car which the Palestine Office had acquired especially for this journey was attached to a train that was ready to depart. Fifty young Jewish boys and girls crowded

---

* The Western Wall, known as The Kotel (or the Wailing Wall) is considered the last remaining wall from the Holy Jewish Temple (Beth Hamikdash), which was destroyed by the Romans in 70 CE. Since then, it has been a holy place for all Jews, where they place a written wish or a prayer and it goes directly to God.

together inside the car. The twenty girls and thirty boys were children without families and without a home. They dreamed of starting a new life thousands of miles away from the terrible war. The children were accompanied by a few adults. Officially, the passengers in the railway car were sixteen-year-old Hungarian citizens. In reality, the group was comprised of refugees whose ages ranged from thirteen to thirty. Bumek was one of the youngest.

Yona never left his brother's side. Bumek was excited about the "trip" awaiting them. Yona, however, understood the difficulties entailed in the long journey.

The train left Budapest. It moved through the blanket of snow falling on the city and turned towards the east. Yona's heart ached. Who knew if he would ever return to Europe and his homeland? What awaited him in this far-away land? All he knew about it came from the Torah. Would it indeed be a "Land of Milk and Honey" for them?

The train passed along fields and lakes. It passed near villages and stopped in different towns. Yona was amazed by the scenery. He had never crossed such a distance or traversed an entire country.

"Sometimes the train stopped for two or three days for fueling or repairs. We slept on the train, we ate on the train and we kept a low profile. It felt as if we caught someone's eye, we might be stopped and there would be trouble."

On the train, new friendships were forged. Yona and Bumek became friends with Moses Steiner from Slovakia who, like them, spoke German. They met Simshon Klaus from Mukachevo and found their common language was Hebrew. Yona also became friendly with a number of girls who were among the passengers.

The first station was Bucharest, the capital of Romania. The stop lasted only a few hours. Yona was surprised to see a delegation waiting for them on the platform. When the children returned to the railway car they had a few sweets, chunks of smoked meat, and other Romanian delicacies. No one among those Romanian Jews could believe that the Final Solution, aimed at the extermination of Jews, had already started in small towns in Romania. In Bucharest, as in Budapest, the Jews in the capital city kept their eyes closed.

From Romania, the train continued towards the southeast. It traveled the same route used by the famous Orient Express which traveled between Paris and Istanbul. The next stop was in the Bulgarian town of Stara Zagora, where the Danube flows into the Black Sea.

The excited Jews of Bulgaria also arrived with cakes and goodies at the train station to welcome the boys and girls. When the train arrived, they showered the children with candy. It was the Sabbath eve and the children were allowed to leave the railway car. Yona and Bumek spent the Sabbath at the house of a pleasant Bulgarian family. There was not much conversation since they did not understand each others' languages but the boys were embraced by the warmth of this Jewish family.

The adults traveling with the train wanted to shelter the children and tried to conceal the difficulties from them. So Yona and the other children did not know that the Bulgarian authorities, who were under the Nazis' influence, asked many questions about the Jewish youngsters who wanted to cross the border into Turkey. The permits presented by Dr. Blum, a representative of the Jewish agency and the leader of the journey, were scrutinized very carefully.

The Sabbath was over, yet the railway car was still not "released." Behind the scenes, intensive lobbying continued, greased by banknotes that changed hands. Another day passed before permission was granted and the refugees' railway car was hooked up to a new train. Everyone felt relieved as they headed toward the border.

On December 31, the eve of the New Year 1943, tension mounted as the train approached the town of Svilengrad, the border station between Bulgaria and Turkey. Their troubles might not be over if they crossed this border, but at least they would be out of range of the Nazis and their allies. "Turkey had remained neutral.* We knew that if we got there, the critical part of the journey would have been completed successfully," Yona recalls.

When the train stopped at the border crossing, the car carrying the boys and girls immediately aroused the suspicion of the Nazi border guards. Soldiers surrounded the railway car and aimed their weapons at the terrified refugees. A German officer barked orders in every direction. He demanded the car be disconnected from the train "until the investigation is finished."

The young refugees were frightened and restless. Dr. Blum hurried off the train and asked to speak "personally" to the German officer in charge. The soldiers shouted anti-Semitic curses. The night was snowy. The youngsters were left in the lonely railway car without electricity, water or heat. Yona hugged his brother and whispered, "It will be alright, Bumek. Let's just hang in here."

Many hours went by before Dr. Blum returned. He was exhausted, his eyes tired. Negotiations to release the car had been intensive and a large sum of money was paid. The passengers waited nervously to see if the border police would keep their word.

After a while, another train stopped at the border crossing. Sighs of relief went through the railway car as it was coupled

---

* In 1944 Turkey severed relations with Nazi Germany and declared war against them.

to the train. More money changed hands and, with a long whistle, the journey continued. Everyone was relieved when the train entered Turkish territory. They opened windows and breathed in the fresh air. "We made it," they hugged each other. "We made it!"

Not long after, the refugees were gazing at Istanbul,[*] the only city in the world to spread across two continents – Asia and Europe. Yona held his breath as he took in the amazing view of the straits, astonishing buildings, palaces, fortresses, bridges, churches and mosques with their towers standing out against the sky. Yona experienced culture shock, much as he had when he first arrived in Budapest, because Istanbul was so different from the European city.

In Istanbul Yona learned the reason for the insistence that only one child from a family be included on the train. "Dr. Blum told me that no one in Budapest had believed the train would make it safely through the Nazi's line. If the operation failed, at least there would not be two victims from the same family."

In Istanbul, the youngsters were also welcomed by friendly Jews, only this time they were lodged in a hotel. Yona had never been in such luxury. He was amazed to see the bathroom and toilet were next to their room. If it were up to Yona, he would have remained there and been pampered for a week. But their stay was only for one night. The next morning, they were back on the train and on the move.

Yona immediately noticed the difference between the fast-moving, well-oiled European trains and the slow, creaky Mediterranean ones. The railway car was now connected to a train from the Syrian-Lebanese railway system, best known for its slowness, delays and mishaps.

---

[*] Istanbul was then known as Constantinople.

January 1943, Turkey: Yona and Bumek Goldreich (third and forth, bottom left), along with the Participants of the "Train Journey," in a photo taken before leaving the Jewish Community in Istanbul, which hosted them after crossing the paths of the Nazis on their way to Palestine.

As the train traveled further south, the snow-covered mountains and European forests turned into barren desert. Temperatures rose and Yona took off his heavy woolen coat as they reached the arid plains of Anatolia and Ankara, the capital of Turkey.

Yona almost lost his sense of time as the train crept along the Syrian-Lebanese railway. They stopped every few kilometers. How many days had they been on the train? A week? Two weeks? A month? How long had they been crossing Turkey?

The youngsters were already used to the border control and long delays by the time they reached the border between Turkey and Syria. Dr. Blum stepped off the train once again. He was equipped with his files of documents and envelopes of money. He returned a few hours later with the necessary permits.

In northwestern Syria, they pulled into the train station in Aleppo. Yona had his first encounter with British soldiers* from England, India and Australia. They represented a world of new languages and faces. After another strict inspection, the train crossed the Lebanese border. A few hours later, the train arrived at its final destination in Beirut, the capital of Lebanon.

Almost six weeks after embarking on their journey, the children finally parted from the railway car that had become like home to them.

Yona remained very careful but he couldn't contain his curiosity when he heard people speaking Hebrew in the hotel lobby. To his surprise, the men wore uniforms of the British army. He moved a little closer and was amazed to learn they were Jewish soldiers from Palestine who served in the British army. They were members of a Jewish combat organization called the Palmach.** Yona's heart filled with pride at the sight of representatives of the Jewish people who were fighting against the Nazis.

Several days later, the final moments of their journey arrived. This was a critical stage. Would their "immigration permits" open the gates of the Promised Land?

The British, who held the mandate over Palestine, put every possible obstacle in the way of the young Jewish refugees.

---

* At the time, Syria and Lebanon were ruled by the British although they officially remained under the control of the French resistance, Free France, which also fought against Nazi occupation in France.

** The Palmach soldiers (a Hebrew acronym for "fighting units") that Yona met were part of Operation Exporter, the operation to free Lebanon.

While they were still in Beirut, Yona, Bumek and the rest of the "travelers," were personally interrogated by a representative of the British secret police. The investigator asked many questions but Yona just repeated the details that appeared on his Hungarian passport. He was afraid that Bumek might break but his brother also made it through the interrogation. All along, Dr. Blum was there to calm and bribe suspicious officers. Everyone in the group made it through.

Yona and Bumek made the last leg of their journey to Palestine by bus. The spirits of the youngsters were high. One of their guardians taught them a song in Hebrew. The first Hebrew song they learned was the anthem of the Zionist Organization.*

As long as deep in the heart,
The soul of a Jew yearns,
And forward to the East
  To Zion, an eye looks
  Our hope will not be lost,
  The ancient hope,
  To return to our homeland,
  The city where David dwelt.

Bumek sang with all his heart while Yona hummed quietly.

The bus approached Rosh Hanikra, the northern border of Palestine. Excitement increased, but so did the tension. The journey had been long and arduous. They had left snow-covered Budapest and crossed their first border into Romania. From there they had crossed the border to Bulgaria before reaching the problematic border with Turkey. They had traveled across the Syrian desert and traversed Lebanon. What awaited them at the last border?

The permit check at border control lasted a long time but at noon on January 19, 1943, Yona and Bumek finally stood

---
* The song later became the national anthem of the State of Israel.

on the threshold of the new land. A wintry sun shone as representatives from the Jewish Agency welcomed them with wildflowers and sweet oranges. Tears of joy welled up in the youngsters' eyes.

"When an adult leaves a country, escapes or wants a change, it is different than it is for a boy or a teenager who has no choice but to flee to another country at the other end of the world," says Yona. "At fourteen, what you see, feel and remember makes a permanent mark on your life. And all this time, the fate of my parents and Eizo hung heavily over our heads."

As their journey came to an end, Yona still shouldered mature responsibilities but he felt the load was lifting. He felt the accumulated exhaustion of the last several months but he still would not let himself sleep. As they traveled towards the northern town of Nahariyah, Yona was enchanted by the lush green landscape of the Galilee that spread in front of them. He breathed in the scent of the flowers and took a deep breath of fresh air. Yona felt he had come home.

The youngsters' last stop was their new home at Beth Olim, an immigrants' shelter in the neighborhood of Bat Galim, Haifa.

The success of the first train led to another rescue operation that left Budapest at the beginning of February 1943. Seventy-two boys and girls were saved on that train. They came from all over Europe – from Vienna and Berlin, from Zagreb and Warsaw. Yona, Bumek and all the youngsters saved by the rescue trains shared their eyewitness accounts of the Holocaust with the Jewish population in Palestine. Yet even there, people found it hard to believe.

CHAPTER SIX

Yona opened his eyes and looked around the room he shared with the group of youngsters that had arrived together. He stretched his body on the "Jewish Agency bed" – a plain iron bed that every new immigrant received from the Jewish Agency. The sun's rays coming in through the window confused him for a moment. Where was he?

A tanned, energetic and alert guide, wearing khaki shorts and sandals, entered the room, woke up the youngsters and told them to go have breakfast. Breakfast?! How long had it been since Yona had heard that word? But on his way to the rich, delicious meal, a relentless concern still gnawed at him. What about his father, mother and brother, Eizo?

Bumek sat down next to him with his food tray. Yona had not seen his brother relaxed and smiling in ages. Yona had struggled day after day to ensure he and his beloved brother had something to eat and a safe place to sleep. Yona felt a heavy weight lift off his shoulders. He no longer needed to hold Bumek's hand and drag him around a foreign city, worrying where they could hide. Now they were safely in the immigrants' shelter in Bat Galim, Haifa on the shore of the Mediterranean Sea.

Through the dining room window at Beth Olim, Yona's eyes followed the white crests crowning the waves as they broke on the beach. Each crashing wave released yet another memory: His mother crying when they parted. His father's words, "The only treasure that can never be taken from you is what you have in your head." The message his parents had sent, "We have reached Mukachevo," and the terror that crept in with the fear about their fate. Could the worst have happened to them?

Yona wandered around Beth Olim. He watched the sprinklers watering the large lawns around him and the green trees casting their shadows here and there. Yona wondered if it was all real. The brothers had survived great darkness and horrifying trauma. They had been separated from their parents and brother. They were torn from a loving home and their quiet life in Turka. After the dangerous, hair-raising adventures they had lived through, Yona could finally rest. He could stop being constantly alert, careful and ready to run. He was able to let go, put his head on a pillow and sleep peacefully.

They were also given three meals a day. Yona and Bumek feasted on meat, fish, chicken, milk, fresh eggs, fruit and vegetables. Everything was organized and safe.

Yona loved it there. He loved the high blue sky, the heat of the sun and the tanned Israelis. They were so different from the scared, dispirited Jews Yona knew back home in Turka. He loved their Hebrew names: Gilad, Gideon and Avner. There was a proud, self-confident sound to those names. They were connected, rooted. The Israelis spoke only Hebrew and mocked those who spoke Yiddish. Suddenly Poland seemed cold, dull, and far away. His homeland seemed like the negative of a black and white photograph.

"Ever since the days at Beth Olim at Bat Galim, my connection to the Land of Israel has been strong, warm and emotional; and it has stayed that way all my life," says Yona. "I loved everything in the Land of Israel – the feeling of freedom, the wide open spaces, and the challenge; the fact that in the Land of Israel, no one was afraid to live as a Jew."

Each day, Yona increasingly felt that he had come home. Indeed, he remembered it been his father's intention for them to reach the Land of Israel. He recalled how his father had taken part in meetings held by the Zionist organizations that were active in Turka. Sender had even supported the immigration of a number of people from Turka to Palestine. Yona remembered how his father had moaned and "apologized" for not immigrating to the Holy Land himself, since he was too wealthy. And how, when Sender was finally willing to sell his property and move to Palestine, it was already too late.

Soon after arriving in Palestine, Yona and Bumek were visited by former residents of Turka who had settled in Haifa. These immigrants had followed Abba Chushi, a native of Turka, who became an important patron in town because of his position as the head of The Histadrut (General Federation of Jewish Labor in Palestine).* The visitors begged for any scrap of information about family members. Yona told about the "actions" and the mass graves, about the cruelty of the Nazis, and about the Ukrainians who had become collaborators of the murderers. Yona told them that not one of the five thousand Jews in the town remained. In Haifa, like in Budapest, they refused to believe his words. At times, their frustration was so great they vehemently accused Yona of making things up.

One morning, a man with a big smile on his face appeared at Beth Olim to meet the brothers. Yona could not believe his eyes. It was his Uncle Fishl. Yona couldn't contain his excitement, and Bumek ran joyously into the arms of his uncle. Fishl Goldreich was twenty-seven years old and was the youngest of Sender's eleven siblings. Uncle Fishl was the first relative

---

* At the time, The Histadrut owned all industrial factories in Palestine, which made it the strongest political force in the Jewish settlement in Palestine.

the boys had met since they left home. Yona and Bumek were no longer completely alone in the world. There was a close uncle who cared deeply about them.

Uncle Fishl had heard there were children from Turka at Beth Olim and he'd gone to the immigrants' shelter hoping to learn about the fate of his family. To his surprise and joy, he found his nephews there. The boys were curious to hear Fishl's story. The last time they heard of him, Fishl had joined the Polish army in order to fight the Nazis. Uncle Fishl recounted how he arrived in Palestine with the Polish Brigade which was appended to the British army. They made their way through Turkey, Syria and Lebanon. Once in Palestine, however, the Polish Brigade began to crumble and Fishl deserted. He settled in the Hadar neighborhood of Haifa, and made his living working at a British army canteen and "all kinds of side businesses."

When Yona described the horrors he had witnessed in Turka and recounted the boys' harrowing escape, Fishl was also convinced his nephew was exaggerating. "It is unbelievable," says Yona in amazement. "How is it that, again and again, everybody thought we were making this up and imagining things – even our own Uncle Fishl? Yet I insisted on telling about it. I was hoping that the reality of what was happening in Europe would sink into the consciousness of the Jews of Palestine, thus increasing the chances they would wake up and do something about it. I was obsessed with telling – not about the gas chambers and concentration camps, we did not know about them at the time – but about the little I had experienced, seen and heard. Yet people thought even this 'little' information sounded like an exaggeration."

Fishl Goldreich became the guardian of his two young nephews. As a "veteran" Israeli, he showed them how to survive in the new country and how to get along in the labyrinth of bureaucracy. After all, Yona and Bumek were once again newcomers in an unfamiliar place.

The immigrants' shelter at Bat Galim was just a transit station. Here, the newcomers underwent a preliminary evaluation before they were sent to permanent housing. The different Zionist parties divided the immigrants and questioned the children. What kind of lifestyle had they lived at home? Did their parents keep kosher? Did they attend synagogue? Did they celebrate their Bar Mitzvah? Were they "very religious," "slightly religious," or "not religious at all?"

There were a number of different political movements active in Israel. The ultra-secular HaShomer HaTza'ir movement rejected all signs of religion. Together with the Labor movement, they promoted the emergence of strong, confident "New Israelis" as the antithesis to the meek Jews of the Diaspora. The HaPoel HaMizrahi movement was considered slightly religious. The Agudat Israel, whose ultra-orthodox members grew beards and side locks, were stricter and more rigid. Representatives from all of these movements pounced on the group of young refugees. Every movement wanted the youngsters to be educated according to their tradition. The more members a movement had, the greater its political influence would be.

Yona remembers how the go-getters from Agudat Israel pursued him. They chatted with him in Yiddish and promised him a gold watch and new clothes if he would declare that his parents were "very religious." Yona refused. His family had indeed kept kosher and prayed in the synagogue, but his father was a modern Jew and a liberal. And Yona identified with his father. Uncle Fishl also advised them, "Don't go to Jerusalem. Don't join the strictly observant ones."

In the end, Yona and Bumek were taken in by the national-religious HaPoel HaMizrahi movement. They were sent by a rickety bus to the religious Agricultural Youth Village at Kfar Hassidim near Kibbutz* Yagur. The institute was established in 1936 as an initiative of the religious kibbutz and Aliyat Hanoar (the Youth Immigration Organization). It was founded by Henrietta Szold,** an American philanthropist who immigrated to Israel. She was a great woman who made her mark on the Zionist enterprise and was known as the "mother of youth immigration." Henrietta Szold personally visited the new children who arrived at Kfar Hassidim and she showed interest in the story of Yona and Bumek.

1943, Kfar Hasidim: Yona (on the right) at age 16, and Bumek (Avraham), at age 14, as orphan teens in the agricultural youth village.

The village's manager was Abraham Michaelis, a "Yekke" (a Jew of German origin). Harriet Szold and Abraham Michaelis

---

* Kibbutz – A unique Israeli collective settlement based on Socialist values of equality between people, and economic and ideological sharing.

** As fate had it, this remarkable woman did not live to see the independence of the State of Israel.

implemented a religious Jewish education that included phylacteries, prayers, the observance of the Shabbat, and eating only Kosher. This went hand-in-hand with agricultural work in the cowshed and the stables, as well as carpentry and metal work. The teachers, most of them German intellectuals, also taught the children a little English and German, and gave them a taste of a general education. The orphans from Europe trained for life on a kibbutz which was considered a safe place for children who had lost their parents and family.

Yona was assigned to the adolescents' class and Bumek was assigned to the children's class. For the first time since their escape from Turka, the brothers slept separately, each in the company of others of their own age.

At the youth village, Yona also had his first encounters with Jews who did not come from Europe. In the dorm, the classroom, the cowshed and the field, Yona met Jewish children whose skin was darker than his own. They were from Yemen, Syria, Egypt, Lebanon and Turkey.

The Chief Rabbi of the village, Dr. David Ochs, and his wife, Gerda, were recruited to teach Hebrew to Yona. He learned quickly, partly due to the Torah lessons he had attended at the Cheder during his childhood. Yona spoke Hebrew fluently within two months.

The traditional welcoming of the Sabbath on Friday nights (Kabbalat Shabbat) was the most joyful moment of the week for Yona. He dressed in a clean, ironed white shirt and khaki pants, which he had received from the "clothes depot." Then Yona joined the other residents of the village as they assembled at the synagogue to welcome the Sabbath with songs and prayers. After that, the Kiddush and Hamotzi (blessings over the wine and bread) were said in the dining room, and a festive, albeit modest, Sabbath meal was served. For Yona, this was a royal delight. The meal was followed by singing and dancing, the Sabbath joy (Oneg Shabbat).

"At the youth village, a new world opened up to me. One week I was in the drama group, the next, chess; and above all, soccer," explains Yona. He excelled at sports and, within a short time he became a leading figure on the village's soccer fields.

Three months after Yona's arrival, another group of youngsters, who escaped on the second rescue train from Hungary, arrived at the village. Yona volunteered to help the newcomers adapt. Seeing the new orphans, whose timid and insecure behavior reflected the terrors of war, Yona understood what a long way he had come in a short time.

The arrival of the "Teheran Children" was also a memorable experience for Yona. The entire Jewish settlement in Palestine participated in the famous rescue operation. Approximately seven hundred children and adolescents were smuggled from Russia into Palestine. They traveled a torturous route through Iran, across the mine-infested Indian Ocean and through the Suez Canal. A train took them from Egypt to their final, safe destination in Palestine. A few dozen of the Teheran Children came to Kfar Hassidim. Living conditions were crowded so the "veteran" children were moved to tents and the buildings were given to the newcomers. Yona spoke Polish, Russian, German, Yiddish, and his newly acquired Hebrew so he served as an interpreter during the absorption process of the Teheran Children. He provided translations, explanations, guidance, and, above all, reassurance.

❦

During all this time, Yona kept hoping that his parents and Eizo were still alive. He prayed they would be reunited when the war finally ended. Again and again, Yona repeated the words that the Rabbi in Budapest had told him about his parents crossing the border and reaching Mukachevo. Over and over, Yona read the postcard, written in German, that the Hungarian community Rabbi gave him. The postcard, the last sign of life received from his father, was already worn-out and torn. The writing was blurred from Yona's touch. Yona had imagined many possible scenarios even as he tried to deny the worst that could have happened. Perhaps they managed to escape the Nazis and were hiding somewhere. Perhaps they ended up in Russia and were looking to escape. Perhaps they succeeded in fleeing to far-away China, Argentina or Uruguay…

A somber young man came looking for Yona in the summer of 1943. Yona recognized the man right away. Yankel was the oldest son of their neighbors in Turka and was a childhood friend of Yona's brother, Eizo. The visit from Yankel was a great surprise, but Yankel's face was serious and grave as he exchanged warm hugs with Yona. "I am not the bearer of good news," whispered Yankel.

Yona immediately knew that Yankel was bringing the last testimony about Yona's parents and his brother. Yankel had met Yona's family in Sambor, a city in the district of Lvov (Lemberg) in western Ukraine. Eizo told Yankel how he and his parents had succeeded in fleeing across the border to Hungary. They had reached Mukachevo and tried to find Yona and Bumek. Sender gave a necklace to a Jew he met, so the man could sell it for cash. It seems this Jew coveted the necklace and informed on them to the Hungarian Fascists who arrived immediately.

Sender, Elza and Eizo were returned to the death trap. At the Polish border station, they were delivered to the Nazis and sent on a cattle train to the city of Sambor. Yankel met up with them in that isolated, walled ghetto. The Nazis were sending thousands of Jews from the ghetto to the death camps. In order to "ease the pressure" in Auschwitz, the Nazis in Sambor started annihilating Jews in every possible way.

Eizo and Yankel soon found themselves side by side at the edge of a forest with hundreds of other Jews. They were ordered to dig a huge pit. Further down the line, they could make out Sender. Next to him, the delicate Elza also dug while the Nazis and their Ukrainian allies shouted at everyone.

Guns were cocked all around, and the massacre began.

Tears filled Yona's eyes. In his mind's eye, Yona saw the rows of Jews shot to death, one after the other. With single shots or entire volleys of fire, the bodies fell into the pit dug by the very hands of those who were murdered. Hell on earth, accompanied by the sounds of gunfire. As Yankel spoke, Yona saw the bullets hit Sender, Elza and Eizo… the stream of blood… their descent into the massive grave that, within moments, was filled up with bodies.

Yankel fell into the pit, but luckily none of the bullets hit him. The bodies of dead and injured people fell upon Yankel from all sides and buried him underneath. When the last of the several hundred Jews fell into the large pit, the murderers moved along the edges, firing volleys into the heap of bodies. Yankel, buried under a mountain of bodies, held his breath. The corpses above him jerked as the bullets hit them. As the killers made sure everyone was dead, the sighs Yankel heard around him suddenly expired.

It took a long time before Yankel realized the miracle he had experienced. Only when everyone left, when the barking and shouts in German and Russian were replaced with the silence of death, did Yankel dare clear a path out of the bodies and the terrible stench of the mass grave. He ran for his life.

"I will never forget," Yankel said in a broken voice. "Here, take a whiff. Don't I smell like a dead person?"

For the first time, Yona allowed himself to cry and he couldn't stop. "This was the most difficult moment of my entire life. The terrible sights Yankel described still come back to me without warning – at night, in my dreams, in the day, out of nowhere. When I sit down with my family for dinner, when I'm spending time with my daughters and grandchildren, in the middle of a social gathering or at the height of a business meeting – suddenly it comes back, unexpected and without warning. It's an open wound that refuses to heal – ever."

Yona and Bumek mourned the death of their parents and older brother for a long time. The bright summer days seemed gloomy and their joy of life diminished. Yona sank into a deep depression that lasted for days. There was no end to his sadness.

※

Sender, Elza and Eizo Goldreich were murdered on the Eve of Shavuot (the Jewish holiday that commemorates the giving of the Torah) in 1943. Eizo was seventeen-and-a-half-years-old when he died. Elza was forty-three and Sender was fifty-one. May their memory be blessed.

CHAPTER SEVEN

The burden of his traumatic experiences forced Yona to grow up fast. He was independent and handled himself with self-confidence. The youth village at Kfar Hassidim offered Yona a good home, education and social life. But Yona was not satisfied with the normal life of a youngster his age. Uncle Fishl, who often visited them at the village and was like a big brother to Yona, noticed this. Fishl worked in the canteen of the British army, but also had many connections in the city and knew he could help his nephew. One day, Fishl sat Yona down and suggested, "Come to Haifa. Learn a trade."

Yona eagerly agreed and they worked out a plan. Yona would finish the school year in the village, then move to Haifa and learn the trade of an auto mechanic. Yona's teachers did not like the idea but wouldn't prevent him from leaving and becoming independent.

The separation from Bumek was the difficult part. Thankfully, Kfar Hasidim was close to Haifa and Yona promised they would meet often.

Uncle Fishl rented a room for Yona in the home of a German Jewish family. Yona shared his room with two other "veteran new immigrants." Thanks to Uncle Fishl's help, Yona learned auto mechanics at the Shachar car repair shop. Once he earned a license, Yona found a job at Hever, which eventually became Egged, the largest Israeli bus cooperative. "As I was the youngest employee, I got the dirtiest jobs," Yona remembers. "But I never complained."

Yona felt good in Haifa. He liked his independence, his freedom and the fact that everything was actually up to him. He kept repeating the lessons his father had taught him: "What you have in your head, no one can take away from you. You cannot live without working. You should study hard." Yona was determined not to be dependent on anyone. He would not have anyone pity him.

Yona felt like he was "out in the big world." He met a variety of people from religious Jews to non-religious Jews to completely secular Jews. And, for the first time, Yona rubbed shoulders with the native Israelis or "Sabras." This nickname was derived from a type of cactus with fruit that are spiky on the outside and soft on the inside.

Yona joined the HaNoar HaOved VeHaLomed movement (Working and Studying Youth).* He felt the movement represented exactly what he was: a young person earning a living while he studied. Yona experienced his first romantic affairs, and he joined local sports teams which played soccer and a beach racket and ball game called "matkot." Yona was active, good-looking, fearless and determined. These qualities made him exceedingly popular among his peers and he became the "leader of the pack." His counselors in the youth movement quickly recognized Yona's natural leadership ability.

---

* The Working and Studying Youth movement was established in 1924 by working youth who united to protect their jobs and their rights. The movement was affiliated with the Histadrut, the General Federation of Jewish Labor in Palestine, which was a powerful, influential entity in those years.

Those who did not know Yona's past could easily have mistaken him for a native Israeli. Yona was like a Sabra in every way. He spoke Hebrew without an accent, strengthened his body and got a sun tan. He assimilated into Israeli life like a fish in water.

His best friend was Gedaliah Moses, a native Israeli whose parents had emigrated from Russia and belonged to Haifa's elite. The two men gathered a large group of native Israelis around them and Yona felt like one of the gang. They fulfilled the vision of David Ben-Gurion, the founder of the Jewish state. Ben-Gurion saw the "New Israeli" as a free person, secular and a fighter – with none of the complexes and symptoms of a Diaspora Jew. "It was an embarrassment then to wear long pants. In order to belong, you had to wear short khakis. The Sabras spoke ill about new immigrants and sometimes even ridiculed them. The Jews from Poland and Romania did not even count. The only ones they considered worthwhile were those who had come from Russia. They were the 'top.'" But Yona was an exception. "The boys used to ask my friend Gedaliah, 'What about Yona? He's from Poland.' Gedaliah would reply, 'Well, Yona is different.'"

The uniform of the HaNoar HaOved movement was a blue shirt with a red lace closure at the neck. Yona wore his uniform proudly and internalized their slogan: "To Labor, Defense and Peace, Rise and Actualize."* Yona stood out as a strong, assertive young man with organizational and leadership qualities. When the position of movement head in Haifa became available, Yona was unanimously elected. He became a local political figure and was considered the head of the Haifa youth. Within a couple of years, Yona was

---

* Quoted from a song by Abraham Broides, the composer of the HaNoar HaOved. The song was written after the violent attacks of Arabs against Jews in 1929.

chosen as the head of the national movement and became the first new immigrant to serve as the leader of the Zionist youth movement.

Leaders of the Labor Union marked the promising young man as having potential for political leadership. Gossips claimed Yona reached the exalted position due to his alleged relationship with the head of the Labor Union, Abba Chushi, who had worked for Sender Goldreich before immigrating to Israel. How else could a new immigrant, who had arrived less than two years earlier, reach such a high position? Yona vehemently denies the charge, "Not only did Abba Chushi not help me, Uncle Fishl also warned me, 'Don't ask that Socialist for any favors.'" Yona got the job on the strength of his personality and work ethic. He set a strong example as a young man who worked and studied hard.

True to the basic values of the movement, Yona entered his position as head of the HaNoar HaOved energetically. He negotiated salaries and appropriate rights for Jewish laborers. He organized jobs and convinced employers to take on Jews instead of Arabs. He led the movement's youth leaders.

Yona's boss was a handsome young man, Shimon Perski, who was David Ben-Gurion's assistant at the time. Later he became Shimon Peres, the Prime Minister and President of Israel who won the Nobel Prize for Peace. "We worked together a lot," says Yona, "but Perski didn't like my independent approach. He wanted me to vote automatically for the Histadrut, meaning for The Party. I preferred to vote for what I thought was best for the country, and that was not necessarily always in the best interest of the Histadrut."

In the mid-1940s, Uncle Fishl used his savings to buy a cab. This was a means of transportation rarely seen in Haifa at the time. Fishl joined the cab drivers' cooperative whose offices were located on Balfour Street. A new career opened up to Yona when his uncle offered him the opportunity to cover the cab's night shift. Yona was excited about the prospect but there was one small obstacle. Yona was only eighteen years old and the British would issue drivers' licenses only to people who were twenty or older. Fishl looked for ideas. Yona did not have a birth certificate, it had been left in the forest when he crossed the border into Hungary. And Yona did look older – why not just add two years to his age? Within a few days, Yona had an identity card confirming he was twenty years old. With his usual determination, Yona obtained his driver's license "on the first shot."

Yona found himself with one of the most desired and profitable jobs in town, a taxi driver. Haifa was located on the slopes of the Carmel Mountains and its steep inclines and twisted streets required a firm hand on the wheel. It wasn't easy to drive in the city but a respectable monthly salary was two hundred pounds sterling and Yona could earn fifty pounds in one night.

His customers were mainly British soldiers serving in the Mandatory Forces. He drove them to bars in the Haifa port and back to their bases. As time went by, Yona acquired a permanent clientele and a number of new acquaintances. His clients included Christian-Arab merchants who frequently went to the neighboring towns of Acre and Nazareth. "Everybody asked for me since I would 'fly' with the cab, getting them to their destination at the speed of light," he says.

1944, Haifa: Yona as a working and studying teenager in Haifa

1944, Haifa: Yona and Uncle Fishlel's cab which he drove to make a living, as well as to assist with the Haganah "Special Division" operations.

Now that he was making good money, Yona invested in another dream – learning English. He studied English at the Haifa branch of the Berlitz language school. Yona was motivated by his father's words about the importance of education and he never rested. He registered to study engineering at the Technion Institute of Technology, the first university to open in the country and the highest institution of learning in Haifa. Yona studied ventilation systems engineering and logistics.

At the time, the university was located near the taxi station on Balfour Street. Yona studied during the day, spent afternoons working on youth movement activities, and drove his cab at night.

During the night shift, Yona became an expert on the seaport's nightlife which was known as "Palestine's Nightlife Capital." The seaport was filled with bars and nightclubs like the Piccadilly and Panorama, as well as restaurants and hotels.

Yona was a smart driver and found creative ways to increase his income. A sharp businessman was emerging. During late night hours, Yona picked up drunken British soldiers who couldn't find their way back to their base. He crammed as many drunks into his cab as the car would carry. He aligned additional rows of drunken soldiers behind the cab and they followed the car on foot. Those riding in the car paid one shilling each and those following paid half a shilling. The only problem was dealing with the passengers inside who complained about the slow driver.

Yona enjoyed every moment of his job as a taxi driver, "I gained confidence from earning my own living. My work exposed me to different types of people, and put me through a number of strange adventures. I gained life experience, learned how to handle myself, what to say and when, what was the right thing to do, and what not."

The clouds of war were clearing and relatives from Poland and Russia who survived the Holocaust began to appear in Palestine. The new arrivals included Reuben, Shmuel, Hana and Lola of the Goldreich family. Most of them settled in Jaffa and opened small businesses including a grocery store, a restaurant, a coffee shop and a wood store. Yona smiles as he recalls, "I had one aunt who owned a kiosk, a small store, in Haifa. Every time I came to visit her, she tried to give me money. She would say to me in Yiddish, 'Why don't you want money from me? There is no shame in it, I'm your aunt.' 'But I don't need any, Aunt,' I would tell her. And I really did not need any." Joined by their extended family, Yona and Bumek felt even more secure and connected to their new home.

CHAPTER EIGHT

The Second World War ended with the allies' victory. As the full scope of the Holocaust and its terrors came to light, the struggle for the establishment of a Jewish State in Palestine became even more important and urgent. Arabs were also attacking Jewish settlements all over the country. The Jewish community united toward the goal of liberation from the British Mandate and the establishment of an independent state. There were varied opinions about the method for achieving this goal. The Haganah (Jewish Defense Forces) continued to be the leading, moderate organization in the struggle against the British. The Etzel (National Military Organization) and Lehi (Freedom Fighters for Israel) espoused a militant stance that included attacks on the British army.

During this time, many members of the HaNoar HaOved joined the Palmach (Strike Force) which was the elite force of the Haganah and the precursor of the Israeli Defense Forces. Yona wanted to volunteer but there was a restriction on the recruitment of orphans. Yona, however, had well-honed skills of persuasion and he applied a great deal of pressure. Yona joined the Haganah and was appointed to the organization's Special Unit which was active in the north of the country.

The Special Unit was established after gangs of Arabs massacred thirty-nine Jewish workers at Haifa's oil refineries. This elite unit combined selected commandos and others who went undercover as Arabs. Yona served in a unit of twenty-six fighters who operated under a shroud of secrecy that has not been lifted completely, even today. There are those who say David Ben-Gurion personally confirmed each operation. The Special Units did the "dirty jobs," including the assassination of local Arab leaders and strategic attacks on the British.

Yona still remembers his commander's words on the day he was recruited, "We don't need people who aren't afraid to be killed. A good soldier is one who doesn't want to die, someone who doesn't want to get killed."

Yona's job included gathering information in the course of his "innocent" work driving the cab but, more importantly, he was used as a driver during special missions. Yona's cab and his familiarity with the streets of Haifa, Acre, Nazareth and the surrounding Arab towns made him a strong asset. Yona knew every road, street, alley, dirt road and shortcut. He took the fighters of the Special Unit to their destinations. After they accomplished their missions, he helped them escape quickly and efficiently. He drove special groups who carried out actions of retaliation against the leaders of Arab gangs active in the Galilee (Northern Israel) and Haifa areas. Sometimes Yona transported groups of assassins. Some of the actions were directed against the British.

Yona participated in the well-known operation that captured Sheikh Nimer al-Khatib. The Sheikh was an influential Arab, one of the followers of the Muslim religious leader, Grand Mufti of Jerusalem, and the head of the Supreme Arab Council of Arabs in the north of Palestine. Sheikh Nimer openly advocated that Arabs should continue the work of the Nazis by exterminating the Jews in the Land of Israel.

Information reached the Special Unit that Sheikh Nimer was to attend a secret propaganda meeting with Muslim leaders in Haifa. He planned to arrive in broad daylight via an alternative route. This was an act of arrogance that could not be ignored. For a long hour, Yona waited in his cab at a curve in the road until Sheikh Nimer's American Dodge appeared around the bend. As soon as he saw it, Yona started his cab and accelerated until he passed the "wanted" car. Then Yona hit the brakes to block the Sheikh's car. The Special Unit fighters who were lying on the cab's floor, jumped up, ran over to the surprised Sheikh and dragged him out of the back seat.

Another time, while Yona waited for his comrades, a gunfight broke out between the Special Unit and British soldiers. A bullet tore through the cab. Yona felt the burn of metal on his right palm as he raised it to protect himself from the projectile. Blood flowed from his wound as his comrades jumped back into the cab. In spite of the sharp pain, Yona quickly put the car in gear and raced through their escape route, with the British shooting at them as they fled. The incident left a small scar on Yona's palm, a permanent souvenir of his contributions to the struggle to establish the State of Israel. Others in the Special Unit in Haifa gave their lives to the cause, three of Yona's friends were killed during operations and battles.

༄

Yona was active in the Haganah but he also worked for its counterpart, the Etzel, in an original and unusual way. Yona felt at home in the parking lots of Haifa's nightclubs and bars. He knew that British and UN Jeeps were a very hot commodity and in great demand for the Etzel, so Yona became a car thief.

Officers in the British Army and the United Nations' Forces would drive their cars for a night out. While the officers were getting drunk, Yona effectively exploited his knowledge of car mechanics. He'd put cables together, touch something here, move something there – and, in a flash, the Jeep was started.

The difficult part was driving the Jeep all the way to the Tel Aviv area on the single road that connected the two cities. A young civilian driving a British military Jeep or one carrying the insignia of the United Nations would immediately arouse suspicion. Yona's luck held and he wasn't arrested as he drove along the curving coastal road, heading south to the secret headquarters of Etzel. In a citrus orchard near Herzliyah, Yona would hand over the Jeep and receive a hundred pounds sterling in return. A taxi cab would take him back home to Haifa. "All in all, I delivered four such Jeeps to Etzel," confesses Yona.

With the money, Yona bought a British Matchless motorcycle. Soon Yona was speeding along the beach and up the Carmel Mountains with his first girlfriend sitting close behind, holding his waist, her hair blowing in the wind.

՟

The publication of the British White Paper limited the immigration of Jews to Palestine and established other restrictions. Survivors of the extermination camps were "stuck" in Europe so it became necessary to smuggle hundreds of thousands of refugees into the country. Yona was a leader of the HaNoar HaOved youth movement, spoke many languages, was experienced with train travel and had acquired vast military knowledge. He was recruited to rescue Holocaust survivors in Europe.

Yona, at approximately 18, Chairman of the Working and Studying Youth Movement in Israel

Thus began the Ha'apala era – illegal immigration to Palestine via the Mediterranean Sea.

Yona enlisted with the Haganah's maritime forces. His task was to oversee the Jewish train that shuttled between Munich and Frankfurt in Germany, and the port of Marseille on the French Mediterranean coast. Yona would gather hundreds of Jews from transit camps in Germany, and board them on railway cars purchased by Zionist and Jewish American organizations. The journey was so secret that Yona paid for fuel in cash with funds he received from the Jewish Agency. In Marseille, the refugees embarked on a ship provided by the Haganah, such as the Josiah Wedgwood* where Yona was a crew member.

1947, Haifa: Yona without a shirt (first from right in the middle row) with his friends from the "Special Unit" of the Haganah organization

Every railway rescue mission was complex and fraught with danger. Everything required complete secrecy so as to not draw excessive attention to the large-scale migration process the Zionists were conducting in Europe. It demanded budgetary planning, discipline, caring for the many children among the trains' passengers, providing food and drink, and bribing officials at border crossings and train stations. Yona was responsible for all this.

"When the refugees were stuck on the train for several days," Yona explains, "I had to feed them all. This was a very

---

* The Josiah Wedgwood was named after a member of the British Parliament who was a staunch supporter of the Zionist cause. He died in 1946, the year when the ship started to serve the Haganah's naval units. During one of its trips to Palestine, the ship was seized by the British. Its passengers were forced to disembark on Cyprus while the ship itself was "held prisoner" in the Port of Haifa.

expensive, complicated and dangerous operation." Yona imposed strict rules and urged the engineers to go as fast as possible to reach their destination quickly.

From his home base in Marseille, Yona ventured forth for several train operations in which thousands of Jewish refugees were transported. Between trips, he helped convert cargo vessels into passenger ships fitted with densely-packed bunk beds.

During his trips to Germany, Yona located his Uncle Leon, another of his father Sender's eleven brothers. Leon Goldreich had vanished from Yona's life during the Communist regime. At the time, his parents told Yona that Uncle Leon was smuggling rich Jews out of Poland until he was arrested and sent to forced labor in a coal mine in faraway Kamchatka in Siberia. When Yona met him in Berlin, Uncle Leon was dealing in the black market. Years later, when Yona visited again, Uncle Leon * owned many assets including a hotel, one of the biggest cafes in the city and a lively nightclub called the Moulin Rouge.

Yona spent a total of ten months in Europe taking part in the illegal immigration mission. "I learned a lot about immigration and its various aspects, and how to deal with bureaucracy, as well as how to engage government clerks and solve legal problems. I learned to manipulate these in order to achieve my goals." Yona received many personal decorations for his work, even from Shimon Peres.

From 1945 through 1948, sixty-six rickety ships, carrying about seventy thousand immigrants, managed to break through the British siege and make it safely to the shore of Israel. "Unfortunately, many ships were seized by the British," says Yona. "They expelled the poor refugees to Cyprus and detained them in a huge camp in Famagusta. Only after the

---

* Leon Goldreich went to Israel in the 1970s and died there of old age.

State of Israel was established were the refugees brought by boats to Haifa, and became citizens in their own country. I felt great satisfaction doing this kind of work with the maritime forces. This was saving souls, simple as that."

Yona's brother, Bumek, finished his studies at the agricultural school at Kfar Hassidim and, inspired by his brother, enlisted in the Haganah. Bumek's task was to guard the control tower at the Lod airport, a duty that later paved Bumek's way into the Israeli Air Force.

On November 29, 1947, the Jewish population in Palestine listened tensely to the radio broadcast of the vote in the United Nations General Assembly on the partition plan to establish two states in Palestine: one Jewish and one Arab. Yona and his friends gathered together and turned their radio up to full-volume. Counting the votes at the United Nations was a slow and nerve-racking process. Every vote counted. With every "yes" vote, the listeners' spirits lifted with great hope. With every "no" vote, a disappointed sigh of worry would escape their lips.

Finally the decision to establish a Jewish State, "after two thousand years of Diaspora," received the required majority. At once, shouts of joy burst from everyone's throats and people began to dance spontaneously on the main streets in Haifa.

The joy didn't last long. All of the Arab countries rejected the United Nations' decision and announced they would prevent the establishment of a Jewish State. The very next day, news kept arriving about people being killed on the roads. Buses were attacked when they passed close to Arab villages.

After the resolution passed, war broke out between the Jews and Arabs in Haifa. The battle was over within only twenty-four hours. The Haganah forces were victorious and a majority of the Arab population fled from the city. On the eve of Passover, April 23, 1948, Moshe Carmel, the commander of the Haganah in Haifa, published the following statement: "Based on my authority and with the approval of the supreme command, I hereby declare an independent Hebrew administration in the city of Haifa."

On May 14, 1948, David Ben-Gurion declared the establishment of the State of Israel, with Jerusalem as its capital. Ben-Gurion was elected its first Prime Minister. One day later, on May 15, 1948, Israel's War of Independence began when the armies of five Arab countries invaded Israel and attacked Jewish settlements.

The fighting organizations joined to form one army, the Israel Defense Forces (IDF). The Special Unit disbanded and some of its members dispersed between the intelligence agencies of the new country – the Mossad (Secret Service) and the Shabak (Israel Security Agency). Yona and Bumek took part in the establishment of two of the most important divisions of the new army. Yona helped establish the Israeli Navy and Bumek was among the first navigators of the Israeli Air Force.

੭੦

The War of Independence was fought on all fronts. The British had left the country and the Josiah Wedgwood, which had been captured as part of the "shadow naval forces" during the Ha'apala, was released from British detention. In March 1948, David Ben-Gurion, who also served as the Minister of Defense, ordered the formation of the Naval Services (later to become the Israeli Navy). The Wedgwood became operational again. The order was given to immediately convert the Wedgwood to a battle ship. Four cannons and four machine guns were installed on its deck. The Wedgwood was ready to patrol and secure the coastal borders of the new country.

118 CHAPTER EIGHT

1948, Haifa: Yona Goldreich (first from right in the middle row) with his friends and fellow fighters in Israel's War of Independence

1951. Navigator, Squadron 103

1951 Bumek Goldreich, Navigator, Squadron 103

Yona had earned an engineering degree at the Technion and had thorough knowledge of car mechanics. He was the ideal candidate to be the ship's Engine Officer. Yona volunteered for service without giving it a second thought.

In June 1948, the Wedgwood went to sea under the command of Arieh Kaplan (Kippi), who later became a Colonel in the Israeli Navy. "Egyptian ships attacked the port of Jaffa and it was our job to fire back and keep them away from Israel's territorial waters," explains Yona.

Yona faced one of his most difficult decisions while serving on the Wedgwood when he was ordered to open fire on another Jewish ship, the Altalena. The Altalena was an Etzel ship. Etzel was a rival organization of the Haganah but by June of 1948, the underground organizations had already been transformed into the country's official army. However, when the Altalena appeared off the coast of Kfar Vitkin, not far from Haifa, differences of opinion erupted concerning the unloading and distribution of the weapons smuggled on the ship. David Ben-Gurion ordered the Etzel to surrender the ship and its entire cargo to the IDF (Israel Defense Force). Menachem Begin,* commander of the Etzel, rejected the ultimatum. A fight broke out between the Altalena and the Navy's ships.

The Wedgwood, with Yona supervising its engines, was sent with another ship, the Eilat, to block the Altalena on its way to the shores of Tel Aviv. An order came to open fire and Yona refused. Yona confronted his commanding officer and informed him, "I will not take part in attacking a ship which carries Jews. This is against my principles and my conscience. Although it's true that the members of Etzel are extremists, they too have been fighting for our independence. We are all Jews!"

---

* Menachem Begin later became Prime Minister of Israel.

A short battle at sea broke out between the Wedgwood and the Altalena. The latter succeeded in escaping to the Tel Aviv beach where it got stuck on a sandbank. Finally, the Altalena sustained a direct hit by a cannon shell that was shot from the beach. The Altalena caught fire off the Tel Aviv shore in a scene that remains engraved in the nation's memory. Sixteen Etzel fighters and three IDF solders were killed in the course of this difficult and tragic confrontation. It became known as the Altalena Affair. The issues arising from the affair continue to stir controversy even today: the need for a unified army, obedience to the government and a basic imperative to prevent a civil war.

The high command ignored Yona's disobedience even though it was considered a severe military offense. Perhaps it was because Yona had lost his family in the Holocaust or perhaps it was due to the influential position he had once held as the head of the HaNoar HaOved. After the Altalena incident, Yona resigned from service on the Wedgwood.

CHAPTER NINE

Yona was twenty-one when the fighting was over. He joined Zim, the national shipping line and Israel's first commercial fleet. Yona participated in the company's first acquisitions. He was part of the team that flew to the United States in order to launch Zim's first three cargo ships, the Haifa, Tel Aviv and Tzfonit. The old vessels were renovated in New York's shipyards, and then sailed to the port of Haifa, stopping at exotic ports along the way. These travels exposed Yona to the "really big world." He was amazed at the powerful energy of New York and became acquainted with port cities in England, Belgium and along the Mediterranean coast.

Yona had acquired extensive organizational and managerial experience during his years with the youth movement, the Special Unit and the illegal immigration operations. He was also charming and a natural leader known for stating his opinions with sincerity and determination. These qualities made Yona an ideal representative for the workers and he was elected to the Workers' Committee at Zim. This position soon placed him in the middle of one of the most famous labor disputes in the history of Israel. The Sailors' Strike caused an enormous public uproar and changed the course of Yona' life.

A labor dispute erupted between the Sailors' Committee and the General Labor Union, the Histadrut, which represented all the workers in the new country. At the time, the Port of Haifa was the only commercial harbor in the State of Israel, and Israeli sailors were subordinate to the Haifa Workers' Committee. The sailors didn't like this forced hierarchy. They wanted to establish their own independent, national organization within the framework of the Histadrut. "The clerks at the Haifa Labor Union took better care of the interests of Zim, which was owned by the Histadrut, than the interests of the two thousand sailors who made the company work and gave it their best," explains Yona. "It was a complete paradox. The Histadrut represented the workers as well as their employers. Naturally, this created a conflict."

The Histadrut opposed the sailors' request for independence. In response, the sailors, under the leadership of Captain Yitzhak (Ike) Aharonovitch, Officer Nimrod Eshel and Engineering Officer Yona Goldreich (all former participants in the illegal immigration), collectively quit their jobs with Zim. As a result, the Histadrut hired foreign sailors to operate the shipping line. "That started a wildcat strike that swept up all of the sailors," says Yona. "Zim used cheap labor from Greece and Italy, and suddenly they didn't need Israelis anymore." The Sailors' Strike, the first strike in the history of the young state, began in November 1951.

Yona was on a vessel loading cargo in New York when he received the urgent message, via telex: "Zim's sailors have decided to stop operating the commercial ships." Nimrod Eshel appointed Yona to be the representative of the Sailors' Committee in the United States. Yona was instructed to make sure that work on all Israeli ships anchored in American ports would cease completely. "Nimrod Eshel led the strike in Israel, and I made sure that it would apply to the ships docking in the USA," recalls Yona.

Israel's government strongly opposed the strike and did everything possible to stop it. Prime Minister David Ben-Gurion announced in the Knesset, Israel's parliament, "There is no strike and there will be no strike. This is an attempt of sabotage by the country's enemies."

Ben-Gurion's office issued conscription orders commanding the strike's leaders in Israel to report for reserve duty, in order to neutralize their influence. This move drew angry responses from the public.

When the Histadrut announced the establishment of a New Sailors' Organization, serious fights broke out in the Port of Haifa between the strikers and the police. The striking sailors were forcibly taken off the ships.

In the meantime, Yona and the Israeli sailors who were striking in the United States had another problem. At the time, a sailor who stayed in the United States for more than thirty days, especially one from a ship that was on strike, was considered an illegal alien, and forced to leave the country. While the strike in Israel was reaching a violent climax, all one hundred sailors in the United States were transferred to the transit station on Ellis Island until their fate was decided. Yona remained ashore, the only person responsible for the ships affected by the strike.

After six weeks of violent clashes, the sailors' leaders, who were still on reserve duty, were called to the negotiating table. The strike ended after the sailors were promised it wouldn't be held against them. The striking sailors wouldn't be fired and would be returned to work on their ships.

The strike, violent incidents and involvement of the IDF in a civilian labor conflict led to intense public dispute and made headlines in all the papers. Uri Avneri, a journalist who owned and edited the outspoken magazine HaOlam HaZeh ("This World") took the side of the strikers and gave them comprehensive coverage. Close-up photos of Eshel and Goldreich, leaders of the strike on both sides of the globe, were on the cover of the magazine almost every week. The story was sensational. The foreign press, especially American newspapers, also covered the strike extensively. Yona's reputation as the one responsible for stopping work on Israeli ships in the United States made headlines in Israel and around the world: "Yona Goldreich, strike leader, stopped work on Israeli vessels!"

The agreement stated, "There will be no retaliation against the leaders of the strike." In conversations with Nimrod Eshel, however, Yona learned Zim prevented Eshel from returning to his job. Eshel was forced to sail with foreign ships. Yona feared retaliation from the Histadrut would hurt him as well. If he returned to Israel, he would meet the same fate as the rest of the strike leaders. On the other hand, Yona was an illegal alien in the United States. The Israeli consul in New York was the one who recommended that Yona not return to Israel until "the storm passes." The consul used his connections and arranged for Yona to receive a visa for six months.

Equipped with a temporary residency permit, Yona used the connections he had made during the strikes to find work with the American Navy. "When I presented myself to the Navy manpower department, the officer in charge, who was Jewish, asked me for my name. 'Yona Goldreich,' I replied. 'Yona Goldreich?' the officer was impressed. 'I've read about you in the *New York Times*. If you pass the security check, you are hired.'"

When Yona had first arrived in America, he found that it was difficult for Americans to pronounce his name. To make it easier for his American friends, "Yona" became "Jona" and "Goldreich" became "Goldrich." So, in the Navy's records, Yona was listed using his new, adopted surname, "Goldrich."

"After I passed the security check," recalls Yona, "I was assigned to a ship named after General Harry Taylor. The pay was pretty good, five hundred dollars a month which was considered quite substantial at the time. The ship I served on carried American soldiers to military bases in Germany. That was part of the treaty the Germans had been forced to sign after their surrender at the end of the Second World War. And on our way back, our ship was loaded with refugees seeking shelter in the United States."

Six months later the vessel stopped sailing, and Yona found himself out of a job again. However, his employment period in the Navy made him eligible to receive a Green Card (a work permit). Yona was fascinated with American freedom and the many opportunities the United States had to offer.

With the Green Card in his pocket, Yona made his way to Boston, Massachusetts. He tried to be accepted as a Master's degree student of Engineering at one of the most prestigious universities in the country, the Massachusetts Institute of Technology (MIT). Yona's English was not strong enough for acceptance to the university. So Yona registered for preparatory classes in order to improve his knowledge of the English language, and to prepare for academic studies. Yona, however, was used to the warm, comfortable weather in Israel and quickly discovered he couldn't stand the rainy, chilly climate of northeastern United States. He decided to give up the idea of MIT and an academic career.

Yona was a young, single man. He was free of debts and not really worried about how he would make a living. He had saved a little money while working in the Navy so he bought a coast-to-coast ticket and boarded a Greyhound bus headed for California, the land of sunshine.

Yona's first stop was San Francisco. He hoped to find work at the local American Naval base but was turned down. San Francisco charmed him, but Yona's money was dwindling fast.

Again, he made his way to the bus station. Yona had only fifty dollars in his pocket when he purchased a ticket and headed for Los Angeles.

When Yona arrived at the central bus station in downtown Los Angeles, he stepped off the bus and his eyes fall upon a banner with huge print: "Every day, a thousand newcomers come to California!"

In the beginning of the 1950s, there were eight million residents in California but more were arriving every day. Yona caught a glimpse into the future. "All of those new arrivals will need a place to live," he thought. At that moment he made the decision to work in the construction industry.

Twenty-five-year-old Yona was once again alone in a big city, but the city of Los Angeles welcomed him. Yona rented a small apartment and looked for business opportunities. At first he worked as a car mechanic for eighty dollars a week, and also installed window screens in new buildings.

"I didn't even imagine myself staying in the States," says Yona. "I thought that things would calm down in Israel after the sailors' strike. In the meantime, I would work, save up some money, and return to Israel. I dreamed about Haifa, sunbathing on the beach, playing matkot, and sitting in coffee shops with beautiful Israeli girls. I wanted to go back to Israel with enough money so I wouldn't have to work again for the rest of my life."

Los Angeles of the 1950s was constantly growing and building. Southern California experienced an economic boom as hundreds of thousands of discharged soldiers chose to live there after the Second World War ended. The city expanded fast and the San Fernando Valley started filling up with houses and apartment buildings. There were golden opportunities for an ambitious young entrepreneur. Yona noticed that contractors, in their hurry to put up buildings, left the windows dirty. Thus, Yona started his first business in the United States, a window washing company.

Soon Yona approached building contractors with another offer. Most of them hired temporary workers to clear out the garbage and waste while construction was still underway. Yona offered to provide the contractors with as many workers as needed. The contractors would pay a fixed price per project. "This way, they would be free from hiring temporary workers and firing them at the end of the job," explains Yona. "I saved them this headache."

Yona's company blossomed. It expanded from cleaning windows to cleaning houses and buildings before tenants moved in. This was worthwhile for the contractors who could give the buyers clean apartments. And it was profitable for Yona. His workers were hired to pick up the waste while construction was underway, and when construction was complete, they would clean up the entire site and the apartments.

It was a good business but Yona was not satisfied yet. "I met contractors and subcontractors, made connections and formed relationships," he explains. "I learned from successful developers and from the mistakes of others, and decided to enter the construction business."

In 1955, twenty-eight-year-old Yona built his first building, an apartment house with twenty-four units. Yona's business was going well and growing. He started looking for a partner, "But it was difficult for me to find a Jewish partner who was willing to join a cleaning business. They didn't understand this was an excellent business. I myself didn't clean anything. I had workers."

Two years later Yona found his partner when he met Sol Kest. Sol became Yona's partner and business soul-mate. Sol managed the cleaning company while Yona invested his time in the construction business.

Yona built apartment buildings and houses in North Hollywood and the San Fernando Valley. He built one after the other, sometimes even several buildings at the same time. Eventually, he expanded to other parts of the Los Angeles area.

"Persistence, hard work and common sense" was Yona's formula for success. Within a few years, he was one of the leading building contractors in Los Angeles. Nevertheless, Yona still dreamed of returning to Israel. "By the age of twenty-nine, I had a quarter of a million dollars in my bank account. I thought to myself that, with such an amount, I would certainly be able to live like a king in Israel. Yet, my brother, Bumek, who was a navigator for Israel's airline, El Al, at the time, warned me, 'Since you left Israel, everything has become very expensive. Don't come back before you've got half a million dollars.'" Yona listened to his brother and set himself a goal. He would save half a million dollars and then return to Israel.

Yona soon saw a new opportunity to expand his business. Until the 1960s, every day after four in the afternoon, the city of Los Angeles was covered with smoke because of the contractors who were burning waste everywhere. The Los Angeles municipality decided this was unbearable. A law was passed limiting the burning of construction waste and garbage to designated, distant locations. Yona purchased several dozen trucks. He organized the transport of construction waste to the collection points in the authorized areas. The cleaning company, Active Cleaning, became the leading company in the field.

At the same time, Yona built hundreds of subsidized housing units, where low-income families were housed, with partial funding from the government. By the mid-1960s, Goldrich and Kest employed more than one hundred and twenty workers.

1960, Los Angeles: Yona Goldreich (now known as Jona Goldrich)

1960, Los Angeles: Jona Goldrich and his partner, Sol Kest, receive an award for their leadership in the field of construction and property management

Yona finally reached his goal of saving half a million dollars for his return to Israel. But fate had other plans for him. In December of 1959, Yona met Doretta Selda Feiner at a restaurant on Sunset Boulevard and they fell in love. He was no longer alone. Yona and Doretta were married on July 4, 1960.

The couple settled in Los Angeles and started their own family. Yona and Doretta have two beautiful daughters, Melinda Elza and Andrea Isabelle. Their daughters grew up safely, in the loving embrace of both parents. As a child, Yona's parents had been torn from his life, but he always carried their love and wise counsel with him. He passed this legacy on to his own children and they carry it into the future. Melinda, the eldest, is now President of the Jewish Federation in Aspen, Colorado. Like her father, Melinda is committed to the Zionist cause. She raises money for the State of Israel and visits there most every year. Andrea, the youngest daughter, also follows in her father's footsteps and joined the Board of the Los Angeles Museum of the Holocaust that Yona helped build. Andrea and her husband, Barry Cayton, are the parents of Yona's beloved grandchildren, Garrett, Lindsay and Derek Cayton.

Yona remains very close to his brother, Bumek, who still lives in Israel. Bumek served for eight years as a navigator in the Israeli Air Force and was discharged with the rank of Lieutenant Colonel. He then worked as a navigator for El Al Israeli Airlines for 25 years. He is married to Bella and lives in Tel Aviv. Bumek* has three daughters and six grandchildren.

---

* Bumek Goldreich told his life story in "The Navigator."

Jona and Bumek (Avraham) remain close at heart to this day

༄

Although Yona's family and business kept him in the United States, he generously donates to the State of Israel. "I am very involved in what goes on in Israel," says Yona. "If it were not for the State of Israel, we would be ashamed of being Jews. Before the establishment of Israel, Jews were considered cowards and greedy. Israel made us stand up straight."

Yona funded the construction of several buildings and facilities at Tel Aviv University, where he also supports the Goldreich Family Institute for Yiddish Language, Literature, and Culture. He has donated to Yad Vashem, the Holocaust Museum in Jerusalem, to Bet Hatefutsot, the Museum of the Jewish Diaspora in Tel Aviv, and to hospitals and other causes.

"The field of education is especially close to my heart," says Yona passionately. "It's important for me to teach the young generation about the Holocaust. The world wants us to forget the biggest horror mankind ever created, the murder of six million Jews by a country that was, at the time, considered the most cultured and enlightened in the world. I am fighting against forgetting. We, the Jews, must support every Jewish cause. We have to contribute to the deepening of our roots and help the State of Israel as best we can."

In Los Angeles, Yona is also an active participant in the Jewish and Israeli community. Yona and several other Holocaust survivors initiated and built the largest monument to the Holocaust on the West Coast. Every year, the monument in Pan Pacific Park in Los Angeles is the venue of a Holocaust memorial ceremony. Yona and the Board's vision was to build a permanent museum in Pan Pacific Park. That dream came to fruition when the Los Angeles Museum of the Holocaust (LAMOTH) opened its doors on October 14, 2010. LAMOTH is always free and open to the public. The museum is fulfilling its stated mission of "providing an intimate environment that commemorates those who perished and those who survived, and educates the public about this horrific episode in human history."

"Every day I ask myself, 'Where was God? Where did he disappear?'" says Yona. "And I also wonder, 'How could a man like my father, a smart, talented businessman, not recognize the danger?' On the other hand, how courageous he was to send his two children to cross the border alone. Sometimes, at night, I can't fall asleep. The images and terrible nightmares don't let go. I think it's all a horrific hallucination… a bad dream. I think I'm making everything up, imagining it. It's inconceivable. How did they annihilate Europe's Jews? Why is there no remnant of the great Jewish community of Turka? Why did I lose twenty cousins? Why didn't any of the children who studied with me in the Cheder remain alive? Why was the world silent? Why didn't American Jews do anything to make President Roosevelt intervene? These questions keep me up at night, and I am worried. Within ten, fifteen years, there will be no survivors left alive. That is why it is so important for us to tell our story."

EPILOGUE

1992 – A lifetime had passed since Yona and Bumek stood in front of their childhood home. A lifetime since the brothers last saw their mother, father and brother, Eizo. Yona longed to be surrounded by his entire family – but that could never be.

More than anything, Yona hoped the new residents of the house had found and kept the family's photo album. Perhaps the album was still in its secret hiding place in the attic. Their cousins, Meir, Itzhak and Steven, crowded close as Yona and Bumek approached the front door. The Mayor and the Chief of Police joined them on the doorstep. Expectantly, Yona knocked.

The door to his home opened but Yona could not enter. The Ukrainians who lived there refused to listen to his pleas. They ignored Bumek. They ignored the requests of the Mayor and the Chief of Police. The name Goldreich meant nothing to these new residents. They claimed they had not found a single thing. They mumbled something about not finding the old photo album or they didn't keep it. Their faces were expressionless as they slammed the door in Yona's face.

The door closed on their last chance to find the family's photo album. Yona was heartbroken. Once again, Turka was a place of devastating sadness and loss for the brothers. But as Yona stood outside his childhood home, he remembered again his father's last words, "Don't let anyone pity you. The only treasure that can never be taken from you is what you have in your head." The photo album might be out of reach but Yona's memories were intact. Time had not diminished the memories of his childhood in a loving home, surrounded by his extended family. Time had not diminished the memories of parting from his parents and older brother. Time had not diminished his sadness at their cruel and tragic deaths. Time had not diminished his memories of Turka or of his escape to freedom. Yona found great success in life but he never forgot where he came from and those he lost along the way. His purpose in life had always been to continue his parents' legacy and bequeath it to future generations.

Yona left Turka without the family's photo album but no one could take away his story. It is his truth to tell. "The only treasure that can never be taken from you is what you have in your head."

THE ESCAPE TO FREEDOM   135

1970's, Culver City, CA: Jona Goldrich, as pictured in the company brochure for Goldrich, Kest & Associates. Today, the company is known as Goldrich & Kest Industries, LLC.

1980's, Los Angeles, CA: Jona (kneeling, second from the right in the first row) and the members of "Jona's Parliament"

*1980's, Beverly Hills, CA: Doretta Goldrich (Jona's wife) with her two daughters, Melinda and Andrea, and her mother – their grandmother, Gertie Baum-Feiner

1990's Aspen, CO, Melinda Goldrich and Andrea Goldrich-Cayton skiing

1994, Marina del Rey, CA: Jona, Melinda, Andrea and Doretta Goldrich on the occasion of Andrea's 30th birthday

2008, Los Angeles, CA: Three generations of the Goldrich family gather to celebrate Jona's 80th birthday.

2009, Los Angeles, CA: The Goldrich's and Cayton's celebrate a special occasion

2009, Jerusalem, Israel: The Cayton Family at the West Wall

THE ESCAPE TO FREEDOM 139

2009, Aspen, CO: Jona's three beloved grandchildren – Garrett, Lindsay and Derek Cayton

2009, Los Angeles, CA: The Cayton Family overflowing with pride as Garrett (the eldest grandson) is called to the Torah as a Bar Mitzvah

2009, Los Angeles, CA: Doretta and Jona Goldrich at Garrett's Bar Mitzvah

2010, Los Angeles, CA: Jona and Doretta Goldrich with their daughter, Andrea, and her family – her husband, Barry Cayton and their three children - in a ceremony in memory of the Holocaust held in Pan Pacific Park

THE ESCAPE TO FREEDOM 141

July 2010, Europe: Jona and Doretta Goldrich (on each end) with daughter, Andrea, her husband Barry Cayton, and their three children, and eldest daughter Melinda, on a summer vacation

July, 2010, Europe: Jona and Doretta on an outing with their grandchildren during summer vacation

142 EPILOGUE

July, 2010: Europe: Jona and Doretta with their grandchildren Garrett, Derek and Lindsay

2009, Culver City, CA: Jona Goldrich sitting behind his desk at the headquarters of Goldrich & Kest Industries

2010, Los Angeles, CA: Jona arriving at Sinai Temple during the High Holy Days

2011, Culver City, CA: Jona Goldrich sitting on the front steps of Goldrich & Kest Industries.

Made in the USA
San Bernardino, CA
26 January 2014